Pearson Education
AP* Test Prep Series

AP* COMPUTER SCIENCE

Fourth Edition

Pearson Education

AP* Test Prep Series

AP* COMPUTER SCIENCE

Fourth Edition

Susan Horwitz

University of Wisconsin

Addison-Wesley

Boston Columbs Indianapolis New York San Francisco Upper Saddle River
Amsterdam Cape Town Dubai London Madrid Milan Munich Paris Montréal Toranto
Delhi Mexico City São Paulo Sydney Hong Kong Seoul Singapore Taipei Tokyo

Editor-in-Chief: Michael Hirsch
Editorial Assistant: Stephanie Sellinger
Managing Editor: Jeffrey Holcomb
Production Project Manager: Heather McNally
Production Manager: Wanda Rockwell
Director of Marketing: Margaret Waples
Text Design, Production Coordination, and Compostion: Integra
Cover Design: Christina Gleason

Many of the designations used by manufacturers and sellers to distinguish their products are claimed as trademarks. Where those designations appear in this book, and Addison-Wesley was aware of a trademark claim, the designations have been printed in initial caps or all caps.

The programs and applications presented in this book have been included for their instructional value. They have been tested with care, but are not guaranteed for any particular purpose. The publisher does not offer any warranties or representations, nor does it accept any liabilities with respect to the programs or applications.

Printed in the United States of America.

For information on obtaining permission for use of material in this work, please submit a written request to Pearson Education, Inc., Rights and Contracts Department, 501 Boylston Street, Suite 900, Boston, MA 02116, fax your request to 617-848-7047, or visit *http://www.pearsoned.com/legal/permissions.htm.*

Library of Congress Cataloging-in-Publication Data

Horwitz, Susan (Susan B.)
　AP computer science/Susan Horwitz.—4th ed.
　　p. cm.—(Pearson education AP test prep series)
　Previous ed. under title: AP computer science A and AB, 3rd ed., 2009.
　Includes bibliographical references and index.
　ISBN-13: 978-0-13-213351-7 (alk. paper)
　ISBN-10: 0-13-213351-2 (alk. paper)
　　1. Computer science—Examinations, questions, etc.　2. Java (Computer program language)　3. Advanced placement programs (Education)
I. Horwitz, Susan (Susan B.), 1955– AP computer science A and AB.
II. Title.
QA76.28.H68 2011
004.076—dc22

2010000167

8　16

Addison-Wesley
is an imprint of

www.PearsonSchool.com/Advanced

ISBN-10:　　0-13-213351-2
ISBN-13: 978-0-13-213351-7

Contents

Topical Review Contents

About Your Pearson AP* Test Prep Series

Pearson is the leading publisher of textbooks worldwide. With operations on every continent, we make it our business to understand the changing needs of students at every level, from kindergarten to college. This gives us a unique insight into what kind of study materials work for students.

We talk to customers every day, soliciting feedback on our books. We think that this makes us especially qualified to offer Pearson AP* Test Prep Series Workbooks, tied to some of our best-selling textbooks.

We know that as you study for your AP course, you're preparing along the way for the AP exam. By tying the material in the book directly to AP course goals and exam topics, we help you to focus your time most efficiently. And that's a good thing!

The AP exam is an important milestone in your education. A high score will position you optimally for college acceptance—and possibly will give you college credits that put you a step ahead. Our goal at Pearson is to provide you with the tools you need to excel on the exam . . . the rest is up to you.

Good luck!

Pearson Education
AP* Test Prep Series

AP* COMPUTER SCIENCE

Fourth Edition

Introduction

This book provides a review of the material that is tested on the College Board's Advanced Placement Computer Science Examination. It consists of the following two sections:

The first section provides topical review. This section has seven chapters, covering the main topics that are tested on the AP Computer Science Examination. Each chapter includes practice multiple-choice questions (and answers) for the material covered in that chapter.

The second section includes some hints on taking the AP Computer Science (CS) exam, followed by four complete practice exams with no duplicate questions. Immediately following each exam are the answers to the multiple-choice questions, solutions for the free-response questions, and grading guides for the free-response questions.

AP Computer Science

The Advanced Placement Program (AP*) offers a computer science exam that emphasizes computer science concepts (e.g., abstraction, algorithms, and data structures) rather than details of language syntax. However, all parts of the exam that require reading or writing actual code will use the Java language.

A complete course description for the AP Computer Science exam can be obtained from the College Board at (800) 323-7155 or via the AP Computer Science Web site. To help you access the most up-to-date information, Addison-Wesley maintains a Web site at *http://www.aw.com/APjava* with links to course description and other useful information about the AP Computer Science curriculum, case studies, and exams.

The AP Computer Science Examination

The exam is written by a committee of computer science faculty from universities and high schools and is designed to determine how well a student has mastered the key concepts in the course. The exam is three hours long and consists of two sections. Section 1 (one hour and fifteen minutes) includes 40 multiple-choice questions. Section 2 (one hour and forty-five minutes) includes four or five free-response questions. The free-response questions usually involve writing Java code

---

* AP and Advanced Placement Program are registered trademarks of The College Board, which was not involved in the production of, and does not endorse, this product.

to solve specified problems. They may also involve higher-level programming tasks such as the design and analysis of a data structure or algorithm, or identifying errors in faulty code.

Both the multiple-choice and the free-response sections include some questions based on the current year's case study (see Chapter 7). The multiple-choice and free-response sections of the exam are given equal weight in determining the final exam grade. Final exam grades consist of a number between 1 and 5 with the following intended interpretation:

5. Extremely well qualified
4. Well qualified
3. Qualified
2. Possibly qualified
1. No recommendation

Many universities give credit and/or advanced placement for a grade of three or higher.

To compensate for guessing, one-quarter of a point is subtracted for each wrong answer on the multiple-choice questions (whereas omitted questions neither add to nor subtract from the total). Students who get an acceptable score on the free-response questions need to answer about 50 to 60 percent of the multiple-choice questions correctly to get a final grade of three.

Within the free-response section, each question is given equal weight. The free-response questions are graded by a group of college and high-school computer science teachers called readers, under the supervision of a college professor (the chief faculty consultant) who has had extensive previous experience as a reader. Considerable effort is expended to ensure that the grading is consistent and fair. A detailed grading guide is prepared for each question by the chief faculty consultant and is used by all readers of that question. Questionable cases are resolved by the most experienced readers and the chief faculty consultant. Students' names and schools are removed from the questions when they are graded, and the readers cannot see the scores that were given for previous questions. To maximize consistency, each of a student's free-response questions is graded by a different reader, and each reader's work is carefully monitored.

TOPICAL REVIEW

1

Basic Language Features

1.1 Expressions: Types and Operators

Every expression in a Java program has a type. In Java, there are two kinds of types: *primitive types* and *objects*. The AP Computer Science subset includes the following primitive types:

```
int    double    boolean
```

Strings and arrays are two special kinds of objects that are included in the AP CS subset; they are discussed later in this chapter and in Chapter 2. Other objects are instances of classes, which are also discussed in Chapter 2.

Associated with each type is a set of operators that can be applied to expressions with that type. The AP CS subset includes the *arithmetic*, *assignment*, *increment*, *decrement*, *equality*, *relational*, and *logical* operators described below.

Arithmetic Operators

The arithmetic operators are as follows:

addition	+
subtraction	–
multiplication	*
division	/
modulus (remainder)	%

All of the arithmetic operators can be applied to expressions of type int or double. The addition operator can also be used to perform string concatenation: If at least one of its operands is a String, then the result is the concatenation of that String with the String representation of the other operand. For example:

Concatenation Expression	Value of the Expression
"book" + "worm"	"bookworm"
"version" + 3	"version3"
.5 + "baked"	".5baked"

Integer division (when both the numerator and the denominator are integers) results in truncation, not rounding. For example, 2/3 is zero, not one; -2/3 is also zero, not minus one. If you want to round a `double` variable x to the *nearest* integer (instead of truncating it), you can use

```
(int)(x + .5)
```

when x is positive, and

```
(int)(x - .5)
```

when x is negative.

Casting can be used to convert an `int` to a `double` (or vice versa). For example:

Expression	Value of the Expression
(int)3.6	3
(double)3	3.0
(double)2/3	.667
(int)2.0/3	0

Assignment Operators

The assignment operators are as follows:

plain assignment	=
add-then-assign	+=
subtract-then-assign	-=
multiply-then-assign	*=
divide-then-assign	/=
modulus-then-assign	%=

The types of the left- and right-hand sides of an assignment must be compatible, and the left-hand side must be an *l*-value. (An *l-value* is an expression that has a corresponding memory location. For example, a variable is an *l*-value; the name of a type or a method is not an *l*-value, nor is a literal like 10 or "abc".)

The last five assignment operators listed above are called *compound assignments*; a compound assignment of the form

```
a op = b
```

is equivalent to

```
a = a op b
```

For example:

Compound Assignment	Equivalent Noncompound Assignment
`a += 2`	`a = a + 2`
`a -= b`	`a = a - b`
`a *= 5.5`	`a = a * 5.5`

Assignments are expressions, not statements; the value of an assignment expression is the value of its right-hand side. This means that assignments can be "chained." For example, the following is perfectly legal:

```
int j, k, n;
j = k = n = 0;  // all three variables are set to zero
```

Increment/Decrement Operators

The increment/decrement operators are as follows:

```
increment    ++
decrement    --
```

The increment operator adds one to its operand; the decrement operator subtracts one from its operand. For example:

Using Increment/Decrement Operator	Equivalent Assignment Expression
`a++`	`a += 1`
`a--`	`a -= 1`

Equality, Relational, and Logical Operators

The equality, relational, and logical operators are as follows:

equal to	`==`
not equal to	`!=`
less than	`<`
less than or equal to	`<=`
greater than	`>`
greater than or equal to	`>=`
logical NOT	`!`
logical AND	`&&`
logical OR	`||`

The equality and relational operators must be applied to expressions with compatible types. The logical operators must be applied to expressions with type `boolean`. An expression involving the equality, relational, or logical operators evaluates to either `true` or `false` (so the type of the whole expression is `boolean`). Expressions involving the logical AND and OR operators are guaranteed to be evaluated from left to right, and evaluation stops as soon as the final value is known. This is called *short-circuit evaluation*. For example, when the expression

```
(5 > 0) || isPrime(54321)
```

is evaluated, the method `isPrime` is not called. The subexpression

```
(5 > 0)
```

is evaluated first, and it evaluates to `true`. Since logical OR applied to `true` and any other expression always evaluates to `true`, there is no need to evaluate the other expression. Similarly, since logical AND applied to `false` and any other expression always evaluates to `false`, the method `isPrime` is not called when the following expression is evaluated:

```
(5 < 0) && isPrime(54321)
```

It will be helpful for students to be familiar with *deMorgan's laws*:

```
! ( x && y ) == !x || !y
! (x || y ) == !x && !y
```

Students should also be familiar with the use of *truth tables*. For example, a truth table can be used to determine which of the following three boolean expressions are equivalent:

```
!(a || b)
(!a) || (!b)
(!a) && (!b)
```

The truth table has one column for each variable and one column for each expression. A row is filled in as follows: First, each variable is given a value (*true* or *false*). Then each expression is evaluated assuming those values for the variables, and the value of the whole expression is filled in. A different combination of values for the variables is used in each row (and the number of rows is the number of possible combinations).

The truth table for the three expressions given above is as follows:

a	b	!(a || b)	(!a) || (!b)	(!a) && (!b)
true	*true*	*false*	*false*	*false*
true	*false*	*false*	*true*	*false*
false	*true*	*false*	*true*	*false*
false	*false*	*true*	*true*	*true*

Two expressions are equivalent if their entries match in every row. So using the truth table given above, we can see that `!(a || b)` and `(!a) && (!b)` are equivalent to each other, but not to `(!a) || (!b)`.

Practice Multiple-Choice Questions

1. The expression

   ```
   !(a && b)
   ```

   is equivalent to which of the following expressions?

   A. `(!a) && (!b)`

   B. `(!a) || (!b)`

   C. `!(a || b)`

   D. `(a || b)`

   E. `(a || b) && (a && b)`

2. Which of the following best describes the circumstances under which the expression

   ```
   !(a && b) && (a || b)
   ```

   evaluates to `true`?

   A. Always

   B. Never

   C. Whenever both a and b are `true`

   D. Whenever neither a nor b is `true`

   E. Whenever exactly one of a and b is `true`

3. Consider the following code segment:

   ```
   int x = 0;
   boolean y = true;

   if (y && (x != 0) && (2/x == 0)) System.out.println("success");
   else System.out.println("failure");
   ```

   Which of the following statements about this code segment is true?

   A. There will be an error when the code is compiled because the first `&&` operator is applied to a non-`boolean` expression.

   B. There will be an error when the code is compiled because a `boolean` variable (`y`) and an `int` variable (`x`) appear in the same `if`-statement condition.

   C. There will be an error when the code is executed because of an attempt to divide by zero.

   D. The code will compile and execute without error; the output will be "success."

   E. The code will compile and execute without error; the output will be "failure."

4. Assume that the following definitions have been made, and that variable x has been initialized.

```
int x;
boolean result;
```

Consider the following three code segments:

Segment I	Segment II	Segment III

`result = (x%2 == 0);`	`if (x%2 == 0) {`
	`    result = true;`
	`}`
	`else {`
	`    result = false;`
	`}`
		`if (((x * 2) / 2) == x) {`
		`    result = true;`
		`}`
		`else {`
		`    result = false;`
		`}`

Which of these code segments sets result to true if x is even, and to false if x is odd?

A. I only

B. II only

C. III only

D. I and II

E. I and III

5. Consider the following code segment:

```
if (y < 0) {
    x = -x;
    y = -y;
}
z = 0;
while (y > 0) {
    z += x;
    y--;
}
```

Assume that x, y, and z are int variables, and that x and y have been initialized. Which of the following statements best describes what this code segment does?

A. Sets z to be the sum x+y

B. Sets z to be the product x*y

C. Sets z to be the absolute value of x

D. Sets z to be the value of x^y

E. Sets z to be the value of y^x

Answers to Multiple-Choice Questions

1. B
2. E
3. E
4. D
5. B

1.2 Control Statements

The AP CS subset of Java includes the following control statements:

```
if   if-else   while   for   for-each   return
```

If and If-Else

The two kinds of `if` statements choose which statement to execute next depending on the value of a boolean expression. Here are the forms of the two statements:

if (*expression*) *statement*

if (*expression*) *statement* else *statement*

If you want more than one statement in the `true` or the `false` branch of an `if`, you must enclose the statements in curly braces. In general, it is a good idea to use curly braces and indentation to make the structure of your code clear, especially if you have nested `if` statements. For example:

Good Programming Style

```java
if (x < 0) {
   System.out.println( "negative x" );
   x = -x;
   if (y < 0) {
      System.out.println( "negative y, too!" );
      y = -y;
   }
   else {
      System.out.println( "nonnegative y" );
   }
}
```

Bad Programming Style

```
if (x < 0) {
System.out.println( "negative x" );
    x = -x;
if (y < 0)
{ System.out.println( "negative y, too!" );
y = -y; }
else
System.out.println( "nonnegative y" );
}
```

Note that the "good" style shown above is only one of many good possibilities. For example, some programmers prefer to put curly braces on separate lines. They would write the above code like this:

Good Programming Style

```
if (x < 0)
{
    System.out.println( "negative x" );
    x = -x;
    if (y < 0)
    {
        System.out.println( "negative y, too!" );
        y = -y;
    }
    else
    {
        System.out.println( "nonnegative y" );
    }
}
```

While and For

The `while` and `for` statements provide two different kinds of loops or iteration (a way to repeat a list of statements until some condition is satisfied). Here are the forms of the two statements:

```
while ( expression ) statement

for ( init-expression; test-expression; update-expression ) statement
```

As with the `if` statement, curly braces must be used to include more than one statement in the body of a loop. For example:

```
while (x > 0) {
    sum += x;
    x--;
}
```

A `for-loop`:

```
for ( init-expression; test-expression; update-expression ) statement
```

is equivalent to:

```
init-expression;
while ( test-expression ) {
    statement;
    update-expression;
}
```

In other words, the *init-expression* of a for-loop is evaluated only once, before the first iteration of the loop; the loop keeps executing as long as the *test-expression* evaluates to true; and the *update-expression* is executed at the end of each iteration of the loop.

Although they can be any expressions, standard practice is to make the *init-expression* be an assignment that initializes a loop-index variable to its initial value, and to make the *update-expression* be an assignment that changes the value of the loop-index variable. The *test-expression* is usually a test to see whether the loop-index variable has reached some upper (or lower) bound. For example:

```
for (k=0; k<10; k++) ...
```

It is important to understand that a loop may execute zero times; this happens for a while-loop when its condition is false the first time it is evaluated, and for a for-loop when its *test-expression* is false the first time it is evaluated.

For-Each

The for-each statement (also called an enhanced for-loop) provides a nice way to iterate over a collection of values. Students should be familiar with the use of a for-each loop to iterate over an array or an ArrayList.

The form of a for-each loop is as follows:

```
for ( type id1 : id2 ) statement
```

In the loop header, you declare a variable using the type of the items in the collection over which you want to iterate. That's the *type id1* part. Then you put a colon, then the name of the variable that contains the collection (that's the *id2* part). For example, if variable allNames is an array of strings, and you want to print each string in turn, you could write

```
for ( String str : allNames )  {
    System.out.println(str);
}
```

You should read the header of this loop as "for each String str in allNames". Executing this loop has the same effect as executing the following for-loop:

```
for (int k=0; k<allNames.length; k++) {
    System.out.println(allNames[k]);
}
```

In both cases, the loop will execute zero times if the array contains no values (has length 0).

Return

The `return` statement is usually used to return a value from a non-void method. For example, the following method reads numbers until a negative number is read, and it returns the sum of the (nonnegative) numbers. (Assume that method `readInt` reads one integer value.)

```
public int sumInts( ) {
    int k, sum = 0;
    k = readInt( );
    while ( k >= 0 ) {
        sum += k;
        k = readInt( );
    }
    return sum;
}
```

A `return` can also be used to return from a method before the end of the method has been reached. For example, here is another version of method `sumInts`. This version uses a `return` statement to exit both the loop and method `sumInts` as soon as a negative number is read.

```
public int sumInts( ) {
    int k, sum = 0;
    while ( true ) {
        k = readInt( );
        if (k < 0) return sum;
        sum += k;
    }
}
```

Practice Multiple-Choice Questions

1. Assume that x is an initialized `int` variable. The code segment

```
if (x > 5) x *= 2;
if (x > 10) x = 0;
```

   is equivalent to which of the following code segments?

   A. `x = 0;`
   B. `if (x > 5) x = 0;`
   C. `if (x > 5) x *= 2;`
   D. `if (x > 5) x = 0;`
       `else x *= 2;`
   E. `if (x > 5) x *= 2;`
       `else if (x > 10) x = 0;`

2. Consider the following code segment:

```
for (int k=0; k<10; k++) {
    for (int j=0; j<5; j++) System.out.print("*");
}
```

How many stars are output when this code segment is executed?

A. 5

B. 10

C. 15

D. 50

E. 500

3. Consider the following two code segments:

Segment 1	Segment 2

```
int x = 0;
while (y > 0) {
    y--;
    x++;
}
System.out.println("x = " + x);
```

```
int x;
for (x=0; y>0; y--) {
    x++;
}
System.out.println("x = " + x);
```

Assume that y is an initialized int variable. Under which of the following conditions will the output of the two code segments be different?

A. The output will never be different.

B. The output will always be different.

C. The output will be different if and only if y is zero just before the code segment executes.

D. The output will be different if and only if y is greater than zero just before the code segment executes.

E. The output will be different if and only if y is less than zero just before the code segment executes.

4. The two code segments shown below are both intended to return `true` if variable `A` (an array of ints) contains the value `val`, and otherwise to return `false`.

Version 1	**Version 2**

```
for (int oneVal : A) {
    if (oneVal == val) return true;
}
return false;
```

```
boolean tmp = false;
for (int oneVal : A) {
    if (oneVal == val) tmp = true;
}
return tmp;
```

Which of the following statements about the two versions is true?

A. Only version 1 will work as intended.

B. Only version 2 will work as intended.

C. Both versions will work as intended; version 1 will sometimes be more efficient than version 2.

D. Both versions will work as intended; version 2 will sometimes be more efficient than version 1.

E. Both versions will work as intended; the two versions will always be equally efficient.

5. Consider the following two methods:

```
public static void printStuff( int x ) {
    int y = 1;
    while (y < x) {
        System.out.print(y + " ");
        y *= 2;
        if (y == x/2) return;
    }
}

public static void mystery( ) {
    int x = 8;
    while (x > 0) {
        printStuff(x);
        x /= 2;
    }
    System.out.println("x=" + x);
}
```

What will be the output when method `mystery` is called?

A. 1 2 1 1 1 x=0

B. 1 2 1 1 x=0

C. 1 2 2 x=0

D. 1 2 4 x=8

E. 1 2 x=8

Answers to Multiple-Choice Questions

1. B
2. D
3. A
4. C
5. B

1.3 Strings and Arrays

For the AP CS course, you need to know about two special kinds of objects: *strings* and *arrays*, and you need to know about both one-dimensional and two-dimensional arrays.

There is an important difference between variables that have primitive types (`int`, `boolean`, or `double`) and variables that are objects. In both cases, each variable has an associated location in the computer memory. However, for a primitive type, the integer, boolean, or double value is stored directly in that location, whereas for objects the location contains a pointer to another chunk of memory where the object is stored. The chunk of memory where the object is stored is allocated using `new`. For a `String`, the allocation usually includes the sequence of characters in the string; if not, an *empty* string (one with no characters) is created. For an array, the allocation includes the size of the array. For example:

Code   **Runtime Representation**

```
int k = 5;
String s = new String("hello");
String mt = new String();
int[] A = new int[3];
```

A `String` can also be initialized using a string literal:

```
String s = "hello";
```

and an array can be created and initialized using a sequence of values inside curly braces; for example:

```
int[] A = {10, 20, 30};
```

creates a one-dimensional array of length three, with the values 10, 20, and 30 in `A[0]`, `A[1]`, and `A[2]`, respectively.

The fact that array variables really contain pointers means that it is possible for an assignment to an element of one array to change a value in another array. For example, consider the following code:

```
int[] A = new int[3];
int[] B;
A[0] = 2;
B = A;
B[0] = 5;
System.out.println(A[0]);
```

In this code, A[0] is set to 2 (and there are no other assignments to A[0]). However, the assignment B = A sets variable B to point to the same chunk of memory as variable A. This means that the assignment to B[0] also causes the value of A[0] to change. Therefore, the value printed is 5, not 2. A picture of how each line of code changes the runtime representation is shown below.

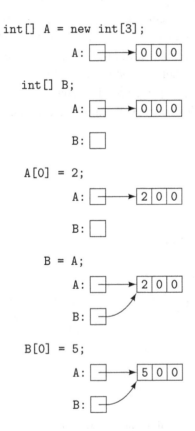

Unlike arrays, Strings are *immutable*. To understand what that means, remember that a String variable S has an associated memory location that contains a pointer to a chunk of memory that in turn contains characters. If you assign to S, you change the pointer to point to a different chunk of memory; you do not change the characters in the original chunk of memory. Here are some pictures to illustrate these ideas:

```
String s1, s2;
s2 = "hello";
```

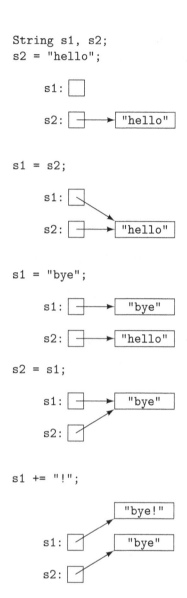

```
s1 = s2;
```

```
s1 = "bye";
```

```
s2 = s1;
```

```
s1 += "!";
```

Note that after executing s1 = "bye", the value of variable s2 is still "hello"; assigning to s1 made it point to a new sequence of characters rather than changing the characters in the chunk of memory to which it (and s2) pointed. Even using string concatenation (the + operator) to change s1 simply makes it point to a new chunk of memory that contains the concatenated string; the old chunk of memory (containing "bye") is not affected.

Every array has a field named length that contains the current length of the array. For example, when the following code is executed, the values 3 and 10 will be printed.

```
int[] A = new int[3];
System.out.println(A.length);
A = new int[10];
System.out.println(A.length);
```

Every String has a method named length that returns the current length of the string. For example, when the following code is executed, the values 0, 3, and 1 will be printed.

```
String S = new String();
System.out.println(S.length());
S = "abc";
System.out.println(S.length());
S = new String("?");
System.out.println(S.length());
```

Because Strings and arrays are objects, they inherit the methods defined for the Object class (see Section 6.1.1). For AP CS, you need to know about the equals and toString methods.

The equals method is what you should use to determine whether two Strings are the same. For example, assume that s1 and s2 are String variables. Then the expression s1.equals(s2) (and the expression s2.equals(s1)) will evaluate to true whenever s1 and s2 contain the same sequence of characters.

A comparison of two Strings using the == operator only evaluates to true when the two Strings contain pointers to the same chunk of memory. Here's an example to illustrate the difference between using the equals method and using ==:

Code   **Runtime Representation**

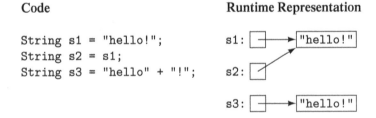

```
String s1 = "hello!";
String s2 = s1;
String s3 = "hello" + "!";
```

Given these definitions of s1, s2, and s3, below are some expressions that use the equals method and the == operator, and the values of the expressions:

Expression	Value
s1.equals(s2)	true
s1 == s2	true
s1.equals(s3)	true
s1 == s3	false
s2.equals(s3)	true
s2 == s3	false

For objects other than Strings, it is up to the designer of the class to write an equals method that returns true when the two objects are "the same." By default, every object has an equals method that returns true only when the == operator would return true; if the designer of a class doesn't write an equals method, the default one will be used.

It is not possible to define a new equals method for an array, so if A and B are two array variables, A.equals(B) (and B.equals(A)) evaluates to true if and only if A and B point to the same chunk of memory. If you want to test whether two arrays contain the same values, you must write code that looks at the values; you cannot use the array's `equals` method.

The `toString` method converts an object to a `String`. When you use the plus (+) operator to concatenate a `String` with another object, the other object is converted to a `String` by calling its `toString` method. Although every object has a default `toString` method, those methods usually don't produce a useful string (e.g., on my computer, the string returned by the `toString` method of an array of integers was "[I7dd0b5aa"). Therefore, if you want to print an array, you will have to write code to do it rather than using the array's `toString` method.

Two-Dimensional Arrays

Here is an example of how to define a two-dimensional array:

```
int[][] A = new int[3][5];
```

When this code is executed, space for a 3-by-5 array (an array with three rows and five columns) is allocated. A common way to initialize an array is to use a `for-loop`. For example, the following code initializes array A so that each row contains the numbers zero to four.

```
int[][] A = new int[3][5];
int num = 0;
for (int row=0; row<3; row++) {
    for (int col=0; col<5; col++) {
        A[row][col] = num;
        num++;
    }
    num = 0;
}
```

To find out how many rows a two-dimensional array A has, you can use `A.length`; you can use `A[0].length` to find out the number of columns. Therefore, instead of using the values 3 and 5 as the upper limits of the two `for-loop` indexes, we could have used `A.length` and `A[0].length`, as shown below.

```
for (int row=0; row<A.length; row++) {
    for (int col=0; col<A[0].length; col++) {
        ⋮
```

A two-dimensional array can also be initialized using sequences of values inside curly braces. One sequence of values is provided for each row, and each such sequence contains a value for each column in that row. For example, the following code initializes array A to contain the same values as the `for-loop` given above:

```
int[][] A = {{0,1,2,3,4},{0,1,2,3,4},{0,1,2,3,4}};
```

Practice Multiple-Choice Questions

1. Consider the following code segment (line numbers are included for reference):

```
1  int[] A = new int[3];
2  int[] B = new int[10];
3  B[9] = 30;
4  A = B;
5  A[9] = 20;
6  B[9] = 10;
7  System.out.println(A[9]);
```

What happens when this code is compiled and executed?

   A. Line 5 will cause a compile-time error because of an out-of-bounds array index.
   B. Line 5 will cause a runtime error because of an out-of-bounds array index.
   C. The code will compile and execute without error. The output will be 10.
   D. The code will compile and execute without error. The output will be 20.
   E. The code will compile and execute without error. The output will be 30.

2. Which of the following statements is *not* true?

   A. Every object has an equals method.
   B. If a programmer does not write an equals method for a new class, the default method will return true if and only if all fields of the two instances of the class contain the same values.
   C. The equals method for Strings returns true if and only if the two Strings contain the same sequence of characters.
   D. The equals method for arrays returns true if and only if the two arrays point to the same chunk of memory.
   E. The equals method for Strings will return false if one String is shorter than the other.

3. Consider the following code segment:

```
String s1 = "abc";
String s2 = s1;
String s3 = s2;
```

After this code executes, which of the following expressions would evaluate to true?

   I.   s1.equals(s3)
   II. s1 == s2
   III. s1 == s3

   A. I only
   B. II only
   C. III only
   D. I and II only
   E. I, II, and III

4. Consider the following code segment:

```
int[] A = {1, 2, 3};
int[] B = {1, 2, 3};
int[] C = A;
```

After this code executes, which of the following expressions would evaluate to `true`?

I.   `A.equals(B)`
II. `A == B`
III. `A == C`

A. I only

B. II only

C. III only

D. I and III only

E. I, II, and III

5. Consider the following declaration:

```
int[][] arr = new int[5][6];
```

Which of the following is an object?

A. `arr`

B. `arr[0][0]`

C. `arr[0][0] * 2`

D. `arr.length`

E. `arr[arr.length-1][arr[0].length-1]`

Answers to Multiple-Choice Questions

1. C
2. B
3. E
4. C
5. A

2

Object-Oriented Features

2.1 Objects, Classes, and Methods

Recall that in Java every variable either has a primitive type (int, double, or boolean for the AP CS subset) or is an *object*. Some objects (e.g., arrays and strings) are built in to the language. When a programmer designs a program, one important question is what new objects to define, and the answer depends on what the program is designed to do. In general, the new objects will represent the things that the program is designed to manipulate. For example, if a programmer designs a program to be used by a bookstore to keep track of the current inventory, the program will probably include the definition of a new kind of object to represent books.

Each new kind of object is defined by a new *class*; for example, we could define the following Book class to represent books.

```java
public class Book {
/*** fields ***/
   private String title;
   private double price;
   private int numSold;

/*** constructor ***/
   public Book( String theTitle, double thePrice ) {
      title = theTitle;
      price = price;
      numSold = 0;
   }

/*** public methods ***/
   // get the price
   public double getPrice( ) { return price; }

   // get the number sold
   public int getNumSold( ) { return numSold; }
```

```
    // sell k copies
    public void sell(int k) { numSold += k; }

    // set the price
    public void setPrice(double newPrice) { price = newPrice; }

    // put the book on sale
    // take off the given percent from the price, but don't go
    // below the given minimum price
    public void putOnSale( int percent, double minPrice ) {
       setPrice( computeSalePrice(percent, minPrice) );
    }

    // determine which book is the most popular
    public static Book mostPopular( Book[] bookList ) {
    // precondition: bookList.length > 0
    // postcondition: returns the book that has sold the most copies
       int bestNum = bookList[0].numSold;
       int bestIndex = 0;
       for (int j=1; j<bookList.length; j++) {
          if (bookList[j].numSold > bestNum) {
             bestNum = bookList[j].numSold;
             bestIndex = j;
          }
       }
       return bookList[bestIndex];
    }

/*** private methods ***/
    // compute the sale price
    private double computeSalePrice(int percent, double minPrice) {
       double newPrice = price - percent*.01;
       if (newPrice < minPrice) newPrice = minPrice;
       return newPrice;
    }
}
```

Every class has *fields* (also called *instance variables*), *constructors*, and *methods*. The Book class has three fields: title, price, and numSold. It has one constructor: Book. It has seven methods: getPrice, getNumSold, sell, setPrice, putOnSale, mostPopular, and computeSalePrice.

At runtime, there can be many instances of a class (each one created using new). For our example, there can be many instances of the Book class, each of which represents one book. If a field or method is declared static, then there will be just one copy of that field or method for the whole class; otherwise, every instance of the class will have its own copy of the field or method.

Constructors

Whenever a new instance of a class is created, a constructor is called to initialize the nonstatic fields of the new object. The name of a constructor is the same as the name of the class, and, unlike the methods of the class, a constructor has no return type (not even `void`).

The `Book` class defined above has a constructor that initializes all of its fields. It must be called with two arguments (a `String` and a `double`). For example:

```
Book b = new Book("The Cat in the Hat", 5.00);
```

Methods

Each method in a class can be either *static* or *nonstatic* and can be either *public* or *private*. A method should be nonstatic when it performs a task that is specific to one instance of the class. Most methods are nonstatic. For example, the `getPrice` and `getNumSold` methods of the `Book` class return the price and number sold for one instance of a `Book`, and the `sell` method changes the `numSold` field of one instance of a `Book`. Therefore, none of these methods is static.

A method should be static when it performs a task that is not specific to one instance of a class. For example, the `mostPopular` method finds the book in the given array that has sold the most copies. It makes sense for this method to be part of the `Book` class (since it has to do with books), but since it does not perform a task specific to one book it also makes sense for it to be a static method. Other examples of static methods are the `abs`, `pow`, `sqrt`, and `random` methods of the `Math` class (a class provided as part of the Java language and discussed in Chapter 6). Those methods are static since they provide operations of general use to anyone who wants to perform mathematical calculations; they are not specific to one instance of the `Math` class, and in fact, you don't even need to create an instance of the `Math` class to use the `abs`, `pow`, `sqrt`, or `random` methods.

Now let's consider how to call the static and nonstatic methods of the `Book` class from code that is not itself part of the `Book` class. To call a static method of the `Book` class, you use the name of the class (`Book`), followed by a dot, followed by the name of the method. To call a nonstatic method of a `Book` object, you use the name of the object, followed by a dot, followed by the name of the method. For example, the following code illustrates how to call a static method (`mostPopular`) of the `Book` class and a nonstatic method (`sell`) of a `Book` object from code that is not part of the `Book` class. Assume that `b` is a `Book`, and `B` is an array of `Books`.

```
b = Book.mostPopular( B );   // call Book's "mostPopular" method
b.sell(5);                   // call b's "sell" method
```

Methods that are intended to be used by clients of a class should be public; other methods should be private. For example, the `computeSalePrice` method performs an operation that is used by the `putOnSale` method but is not intended to be used by clients of the `Book` class. Therefore, the `computeSalePrice` method is a private method. All of the other `Book` methods are public methods.

Parameters

Each method has zero or more *parameters,* sometimes referred to as *formal parameters.* The corresponding values used in a call to the method are called *arguments* or *actual parameters.* A method call must include one argument for each of the method's parameters, and the type of each argument must match the type of the corresponding parameter. For example, in the Book class, the computeSalePrice method has two formal parameters, an int and a double. The putOnSale method calls computeSalePrice with two arguments: percent and minPrice, which are of type int and double, respectively (matching the types of the corresponding parameters).

In Java, all arguments are passed by *value*. This means that what is actually passed is a *copy* of the argument, made when the method is called. Therefore, changes made to the formal parameter by the method have no effect on the argument (since the changes are applied to the copy). For example, suppose we change the computeSalePrice method so that it has three parameters instead of two, where the third parameter is the current price of the book, and instead of returning the sale price, it simply sets the third parameter to that value.

```
private static void computeSalePrice(int percent, double minPrice
                                     double bookPrice) {
   double newPrice = price - percent*.01;
   if (newPrice < minPrice) newPrice = minPrice;
   bookPrice = newPrice;
}
```

And suppose we change the call in the putOnSale method to:

```
computeSalePrice(percent, minPrice, price);
```

In this case, the putOnSale method has no effect on the book's price. This is because when method computeSalePrice is called, the value of the argument price is copied into a new location (called bookPrice), and it is the copy that is assigned to. When method computeSalePrice returns, the book's price field still contains its original value.

However, remember that if an argument is an object, then what is copied is a pointer to the chunk of memory where the object is stored. Changing the formal parameter itself will not affect the corresponding argument, but changing the value *pointed to* by the formal parameter will also change the value pointed to by the argument (since both the argument and the formal parameter point to the same chunk of memory).

Here is some example code to illustrate these ideas:

```
public void changeBook( book b ) {
   b.putOnSale(10, 0.0);
   b = null;
}

public void test( ) {
   Book myBook = new Book("Birds", 10.00);
   changeBook( myBook );
   System.out.println( myBook.getPrice() );
}
```

When this code executes, the Book constructor initializes the price of myBook to $10.00. When method changeBook is called, the value of the argument myBook is copied into a new location (called b). That value is a pointer to the chunk of memory that holds the Book object, including its three fields. When changeBook changes the price of b to $9 (by calling putOnSale), it changes the value of the price field that is part of that chunk of memory. Since argument myBook is pointing to that same chunk of memory, the value of myBook.price is also changed, and so the value "9.0" is printed after changeBook returns. However, the last statement in changeBook (which sets b to null) changes the value only in the location named b; it has no effect on argument myBook, and so there is no NullPointerException when myBook.getPrice is called.

Here are some pictures to illustrate better what happens at runtime:

1. when ChangeBook is first called

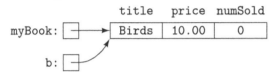

2. after executing b.putOnSale(10, 0.0)

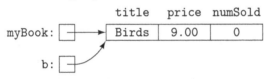

3. after executing b = null

Since arrays are also objects, the same ideas apply to array parameters, as illustrated at the top of the next page.

Return Type

Every method (except a constructor) has a *return type*. In general, if a method is designed to perform some action rather than to compute a value, its return type should be void; otherwise, its return type should be the type of the value it is intended to compute. For example, in the Book class, method putOnSale has return type void because its purpose is to modify the book's price, not to compute and return a value. In contrast, the purposes of method mostPopular are to determine which book in the given array has sold the most copies and to return that book. Therefore, its return type is Book.

Code	What Happens at Runtime

```
public void changeArray( int[] B ) {
   B[0] += 5;
   B = null;
}


public void test( ) {
   int[] A = new int[3];
   A[0] = 1;
   changeArray( A );
   System.out.println( A[0] );
}
```

when `ChangeArray` is first called

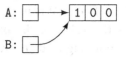

after executing `B[0] += 5`

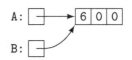

after executing `B = null`

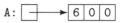

Preconditions and Postconditions

It is a good idea to provide documentation for each method that explains what it does. One good way to do this is to write a precondition and a postcondition for each method. The precondition says what is expected to be true when the method is called, and the postcondition says what will be true when the method returns, assuming that the expectations of the precondition are met. For example, the `mostPopular` method of the Book class (shown again below) has a precondition and a postcondition.

```
public static Book mostPopular( Book[] bookList ) {
// precondition: bookList.length > 0
// postcondition: returns the book that has sold the most copies
   int bestNum = bookList[0].numSold;
   int bestIndex = 0;
   for (int j=1; j<bookList.length; j++ ) {
      if (bookList[j].numSold > bestNum) {
         bestNum = bookList[j].numSold;
         bestIndex = j;
      }
   }
   return bookList[bestIndex];
}
```

It is the responsibility of the programmer who includes calls to `mostPopular` to make sure that the method's precondition is satisfied on every call; if the array argument has length 0, the programmer cannot expect the method to work as intended. In this case, an `IndexOutOfBoundsException` would occur. In general, if a method's preconditions are not satisfied, the method might return the wrong value, perform the wrong task, or throw an exception.

Recursion

A method that can call itself, either directly or indirectly (e.g., by calling another method that calls another method that calls the first method), is called a *recursive* method.

Recursive methods are sometimes much easier to understand than the equivalent nonrecursive code would be. For example, students should be familiar with the Merge Sort algorithm, which is best defined using recursion.

It is important to remember that every recursive method must have a "base case"—a test that can prevent the method from calling itself again; otherwise, a runtime error will occur (e.g., a StackOverflowError exception might be thrown). This is usually referred to as an *infinite recursion*, though in fact the limited resources of the computer prevent it from actually being infinite.

Here is an example of a recursive method that does not have a base case:

```
public void printInt( int k ) {
   System.out.print( k + " " );
   printInt( k+1 );
}
```

If printInt is originally called like this:

```
printInt( 1 );
```

the output will be:

```
1 2 3 4 5 6 7 8 9 10 11 ...
```

and eventually there will be a runtime error.

Not only must a recursive method include a base case, but it must also "make progress" toward the base case, so that eventually there are no more recursive calls. Here is another version of printInt:

```
public void printInt( int k ) {
   if (k < 1) {
      System.out.println( );
   }
   else {
      System.out.print( k + " " );
      printInt( k+1 );
   }
}
```

This version *does* include a base case (the recursive call is not made if k is less than one); however, if printInt is originally called with an argument that is greater than or equal to one, the base case is never reached, and there is still an infinite recursion.

Here is a version of printInt that never causes an infinite recursion, no matter how it is originally called:

```
public void printInt( int k ) {
// postcondition: prints the numbers from k to 10,
//                ending with a new line.
   if (k > 10) {
      System.out.println( );
   }
   else {
      System.out.print( k + " " );
      printInt( k+1 );
   }
}
```

It is also important to understand that a recursive method may do some things before the recursive call and may do some more things after the recursive call. The things that are done *after* the recursive call must wait until all of the recursion has finished. For example, consider the two methods shown below (assume that readInt reads one integer value).

```
void echoInput( ) {
   int k;
   k = readInt( );
   if (k != 0) {
      System.out.print( k + " " );
      echoInput( );
   }
}

void reverseInput( ) {
   int k;
   k = readInt( );
   if (k != 0) {
      reverseInput( );
      System.out.print( k + " " );
   }
}
```

The only difference between echoInput and reverseInput is that echoInput prints the value of variable k *before* the recursive call, and reverseInput prints the value *after* the recursive call. However, that is a very important difference! Because reverseInput waits to print the value of k until after the recursive call has finished, the first value read in to k will be the *last* value printed. For example, if the two methods are each called with the input 1 2 3 4 0, the output of echoInput will be 1 2 3 4, and the output of reverseInput will be 4 3 2 1.

Overloading

In Java, it is possible for a class to have multiple versions of a method with the same name. Such methods are called *overloaded* methods. Two versions of a method must have different *signatures*; that is, they must either have a different number of parameters or at least one parameter must have different types in the two versions of the method (it is *not* good enough for the two versions to have different return types).

Overloading is useful when you want to provide the same operation on different kinds of objects. For example, you might want to define a max method for integers and for decimal numbers. You can do this via overloading as follows:

```java
public int max( int x, int y ) {
    if (x >= y) return x;
    return y;
}


public double max( double x, double y ) {
    if (x >= y) return x;
    return y;
}
```

In this example, both versions of max have the same number of parameters, but the types of the two parameters differ in each of the versions, so this is legal overloading.

Another reason for using overloaded methods is to provide the same operation with a different number of parameters. For example, you might want to define another version of max that returns the maximum of *three* given integer values rather than two:

```java
public int max( int x, int y, int z ) {
    if (x >= y) return max(x, z);
    else return max(y, z);
}
```

The constructors for a class can also be overloaded. When an instance of a class is created using new, the number and types of the arguments are used to determine which constructor is called.

For example, the Book class has a constructor with two parameters (the title and price of the new book). That constructor is called when a new Book is created like this:

```java
Book b = new Book( "Happy Days", 22.50);
```

We could define a second constructor, with just one parameter (the title) that initializes the price to some default value. The constructor could be defined like this:

```java
public Book( String theTitle ) {
    title = theTitle;
    price = 20.00;
    numSold = 0;
}
```

This new constructor would be called when a Book was created like this:

```
Book b = new Book("Happy Days");
```

Although it is not appropriate for the Book class, a constructor with *no* parameters can also be defined. (This kind of constructor is called the *default* or *no-argument* constructor.) If the Book class had a default constructor, it would be called like this:

```
Book b = new Book( );
```

Practice Multiple-Choice Questions

Questions 1 and 2 concern the following (incomplete) Point class.

```
public class Point {
  /*** fields ***/
     private int xCoord;  // the current x coordinate
     private int yCoord;  // the current y coordinate

  /*** constructors ***/
   // default constructor: initialize the point to 0,0
     public Point( ) { ... }

   // another constructor: initialize the point to x,y
     public Point(int x, int y) { ... }

  /*** methods ***/
   // set the x coordinate to the given value
     public void setX(int x) { ... }

   // set the y coordinate to the given value
     public void setY(int y) { ... }

   // return the x coordinate
     public int getX( ) { ... }

   // return the y coordinate
     public int getY( ) { ... }

   // move the point horizontally d units
     public void moveHorizontal(int d) { ... }

   // move the point vertically d units
     public void moveVertical(int d) { ... }
}
```

1. Assume that P is a `Point` variable in a method that is *not* in the `Point` class. Which of the following code segments correctly sets P to represent the point (5,5)?

Segment I	**Segment II**	**Segment III**
`P = new Point();`	`P = new Point();`	`P = new Point(5,5);`
`P.xCoord = 5;`	`P.setX(5);`	
`P.yCoord = 5;`	`P.setY(5);`	

   A. I only

   B. II only

   C. III only

   D. I and II

   E. II and III

2. Assume that P is a `Point` variable that represents the point (x,y) in a method that is *not* in the `Point` class. Which of the following code segments correctly changes P to represent the point (y,x)?

   A. `P.getX() = P.getY();`
      `P.getY() = P.getX();`

   B. `P.setX(P.getY());`
      `P.setY(P.getX());`

   C. `P.moveHorizontal(P.getY());`
      `P.moveVertical(P.getX());`

   D. `int tmp = P.xCoord;`
      `P.xCoord = P.yCoord;`
      `P.yCoord = tmp;`

   E. `int tmp = P.getX();`
      `P.setX(P.getY());`
      `P.setY(tmp);`

3. Which of the following best describes the purpose of a method's pre- and postconditions?

   A. They provide information to the programmer about what the method is intended to do.

   B. They provide information to the programmer about how the method is implemented.

   C. They provide information to the compiler that permits it to generate better code.

   D. They provide information to the compiler that makes type checking easier.

   E. They permit the method to be in a different file than the code that calls the method.

4. Consider the following code segment:

```
public void changeParams( int k, int[] A, String s ) {
    k++;
    A[0]++;
    s += "X";
}

public void print( ) {
    int k = 0;
    int[] A = {10, 20};
    String s = "aaa";

    changeParams(k, A, s);
    System.out.println(k + " " + A[0] + " " + s);
}
```

What is output when method `print` is called?

A. 0 10 aaa

B. 1 10 aaaX

C. 0 11 aaa

D. 1 11 aaaX

E. 0 11 aaaX

5. Consider the following code segment:

```
public void mystery( int j, int k ) {
    if (j != k) mystery( j+1, k );
}
```

Which of the following best characterizes the conditions under which the call `mystery( x, y )` leads to an infinite recursion?

A. All conditions

B. No conditions

C. x < y

D. x > y

E. x == y

Answers to Multiple-Choice Questions

1. E
2. E
3. A
4. C
5. D

2.2   Inheritance and Polymorphism

Inheritance is used in a Java program when the objects manipulated by the program form a natural hierarchy using an "*is-a*" relationship. For example, suppose we want to design a program for a bookstore that sells different kinds of books, including children's books and textbooks. A children's book *is a* book, and so is a textbook. Therefore, we might want to define classes ChildrensBook and TextBook as *subclasses* of the Book class (and the Book class will then be the *superclass* of both the ChildrensBook and TextBook classes).

A subclass is defined using the keyword extends as follows:

```
public class ChildrensBook extends Book {
    ⋮
}

public class TextBook extends Book {
    ⋮
}
```

An advantage of defining classes this way is that subclasses *inherit* all of the fields and methods of their superclasses (but not the constructors, which are discussed below). For example, since every book has a title, a price, and the number of copies sold, there is no need to include those fields in the definitions of the ChildrensBook and TextBook classes; they will be inherited automatically. Similarly, there is no need to redefine the getPrice, getNumSold, sell, setPrice, putOnSale, mostPopular, and computeSalePrice methods; every ChildrensBook and every TextBook will have those methods.

Note that the relationship between a book and a title is a "*has-a*" relationship (a book *has a* title), not an "*is-a*" relationship. That is why title is a field, not a subclass, of a Book.

Usually, a subclass will define some new fields and/or methods that are not defined by its superclass. For example, a ChildrensBook might include the age of the children for whom it is intended, and a TextBook might include the name of the course for which it is required:

```
public class ChildrensBook extends Book {
   /*** new field ***/
      private int childsAge;

   /*** new method ***/
      public int getAge() { return childsAge; }
}
public class TextBook extends Book {
   /*** new field ***/
      private String requiredBy;

   /*** new method ***/
      public String getRequiredBy( ) { return requiredBy; }
}
```

Constructors

As mentioned earlier, the constructors of a superclass are *not* inherited by its subclasses. However, a subclass's constructors always call a superclass constructor, either explicitly or implicitly. A superclass constructor is called explicitly using `super`. For example, we could define a constructor for the `ChildrensBook` class to include an explicit call to the `Book` constructor like this:

```
public ChildrensBook(String theTitle, double price, int age) {
    super(theTitle, price);
    childsAge = age;
}
```

When this `ChildrensBook` constructor is called, it first calls the `Book` constructor to initialize the `title`, `price`, and `numSold` fields; it then initializes the `childsAge` field itself. Since the `title`, `price`, and `numSold` fields are all *private* fields of the `Book` class, they can only be initialized using the `Book` constructor; the `ChildrensBook` constructor cannot assign to those fields.

Note that if an explicit call to the superclass's constructor is included, it must be the *first* statement in the subclass's constructor. If a subclass's constructor does not include an explicit call to one of its superclass's constructors, then there will be an *implicit* call to the superclass's default constructor (i.e., the compiler will add a call). If the superclass does not have a default constructor, this implicit call will cause a compile-time error. For example, if we failed to include an explicit call to `super` in the `ChildrensBook` or `TextBook` constructors, we would get a compile-time error since the `Book` class has no default constructor.

Using a Subclass Instead of a Superclass

Another advantage of using inheritance is that you can use a subclass object anywhere that a superclass object is expected. For example, because every textbook *is a* book, any method that has a parameter of type `Book` can be called with an argument of type `TextBook`; you do not have to write two versions of the method, one for `Book` parameters and the other for `TextBook` parameters. For example, the following method determines whether two books have the same price:

```
public static boolean samePrice( Book b1, Book b2 ) {
    return(b1.getPrice() == b2.getPrice());
}
```

The method will work just fine if both b1 and b2 have type `Book`, if both have type `TextBook`, or if one is a `Book` and the other is a `TextBook`.

```
Book b1 = ...
Book b2 = ...
TextBook tb1 = ...
TextBook tb2 = ...
boolean result = samePrice(b1, b2);   // 2 Book arguments
result2 = samePrice(tb1, tb2);        // 2 TextBook arguments
result3 = samePrice(b1, tb1);         // 1 Book and 1 TextBook
```

The fact that you can call the `samePrice` method with Book arguments or with arguments that are any subclass of Book is one example of *polymorphism* in Java: a method whose parameters can have different types on different calls is a *polymorphic method*.

Because you can use a TextBook anywhere that a Book is expected, not only can you pass a TextBook argument to a method with a Book parameter, you can also assign from a TextBook to a Book (because a Book is expected on the right-hand side of the =, and a TextBook *is a* Book). For example:

```
TextBook tb = ...
Book b = tb;            // assign from a TextBook to a Book
```

Although a subclass object can be used anywhere a superclass object is expected, the reverse is not true: In general, you cannot use a superclass object where a subclass object is expected. For example, you cannot call a method that has a TextBook parameter with a Book argument, and you cannot assign from a Book to a TextBook. To illustrate this, assume that the following method has been defined in the TextBook class:

```
public static boolean sameClass( TextBook tb1, TextBook tb2 ) {
    return ((tb1.requiredBy).equals(tb2.requiredBy));
}
```

The following code would cause two compile-time errors, as noted in the comments:

```
Book b = ...
TextBook tb = b; // compile-time error!
                 // can't assign from a Book to a TextBook
if (TextBook.sameClass( b, tb )) ... // compile-time error!
                                     // can't use a Book argument
                                     // when the corresponding
                                     // parameter is a TextBook
```

If you know that a particular Book variable is actually pointing to a TextBook object, then you can use a *class cast* to tell the compiler that it is OK to use that variable where a TextBook is expected. For example:

```
Book b = new TextBook(...);    // b points to a TextBook object
TextBook tb;

tb = (TextBook)b;                               // no compile-time error
if (TextBook.sameClass( (TextBook)b, tb )) ... // no compile-time error
```

Although the use of a class cast prevents a compile-time error, a runtime check is still performed to make sure that the Book variable is really pointing to a TextBook object. If not, an exception is thrown. For example:

```
Book b = new Book(...);  // b points to a Book object
TextBook tb;

tb = (TextBook)b; // runtime error!
                 // b points to a Book, not a TextBook
if (TextBook.sameClass( (TextBook)b, tb )) ... // runtime error!
                                        // b points to a Book,
                                        // not a TextBook
```

Overloading Methods

Just as a class can define *overloaded* methods (methods with the same name but different signatures), a subclass can overload a method of its superclass by defining a method with the same name but a different signature. For example, the designer of the ChildrensBook class might want a second version of the putOnSale method that just specifies the percent discount, without any minimum price. It can be implemented by calling the original putOnSale method with a minimum price of 0.0 as shown below.

```
// overload the putOnSale method
public void putOnSale(int percent) {
    putOnSale(percent, 0.0);
}
```

Overriding Methods

In addition to overloading methods defined by its superclass, a subclass can also *override* a superclass method; that is, it can define a new version of the method specialized to work on subclass objects. A superclass method is overridden when the subclass defines a method with exactly the same name, the same number of parameters, the same types of parameters, and the same return type as the method in the superclass.

For example, there might be a rule that textbooks for Physics 101 are never put on sale. In that case, the TextBook class might override the Book class's definition of the putOnSale method as follows:

```
// put the book on sale if it is NOT for Physics 101
public void putOnSale( int percent, double minPrice ) {
    if (requiredBy.equals("Physics 101")) {
        System.out.println("Books for Physics 101 cannot be on sale.");
    else {
        super.putOnSale(percent, minPrice);
    }
}
```

Note that if the textbook is *not* for Physics 101, the TextBook method calls the putOnSale method of the Book class (its superclass) to set the sale price.

As discussed above, a variable of type Book may actually point to a Book object, a TextBook object, or a ChildrensBook object. The type of the object actually pointed to (not the declared type of the variable) is what determines which version of an overridden method is called. For example:

```
Book b = new Book(...);
Book cb = new ChildrensBook(...);
Book tb = new TextBook(...);

b.putOnSale(10, 15.50);  // b points to a Book object, so the Book
                         // class's putOnSale method is called
cb.putOnSale(10, 15.50); // cb points to a ChildrensBook object;
                         // the putOnSale method was not overridden
                         // in the ChildrensBook class, so the Book
                         // class's putOnSale method is called
tb.putOnSale(10, 15.50); // tb points to a TextBook object;
                         // the putOnSale method was overridden in
                         // the TextBook class, so the TextBook
                         // class's putOnSale method is called
```

In this example, variables b, cb, and tb are all declared to be of type Book. However, cb is initialized to point to a ChildrensBook, and tb is initialized to point to a TextBook. The calls b.putOnSale(10, 15.50) and cb.putOnSale(10, 15.50) cause the Book class's putOnSale method to be called (because b points to a Book, and because cb points to a ChildrensBook and the ChildrensBook class does not override the putOnSale method). The call tb.putOnSale(10, 15.50) causes the TextBook class's putOnSale method to be called (because tb points to a TextBook, and that class *does* override the putOnSale method).

As illustrated on the previous page, the types of the objects pointed to by variables b, cb, and tb determine which version of the putOnSale method is called. This is an example of *dynamic dispatch,* and it is another aspect of Java that makes it a *polymorphic* language. The first polymorphic aspect of Java, discussed earlier in this section, was that a method's parameters could have different types on different calls. Here we see that a language is also polymorphic if the way an object is processed can depend on its type.

Abstract Methods and Classes

Suppose you want to define a class hierarchy in which some method needs to be provided by all subclasses, but there is no reasonable default version (i.e., it is not possible to define a version of the method in the superclass that makes sense for the subclasses). For example, you might define a Shape class with three subclasses: Circle, Square, and Rectangle. A Circle will have fields that specify the coordinates of its center and its radius. A Square will have fields that specify the coordinates of its upper-left corner and the length of one side.

A `Rectangle` will have fields that specify the coordinates of its upper-left corner, its height, and its width.

It will be useful to have a `Draw` method for all `Shapes`; however, there is no reasonable `Draw` method that will work for a `Circle`, a `Square`, and a `Rectangle`. This is a time to use an *abstract method*: a method that is *declared* in a class but defined only in a subclass. (For our example, the `Draw` method will be the abstract method; it will be declared in the `Shape` class, and it will be defined in each of the three subclasses: `Circle`, `Square`, and `Rectangle`.)

Here's the syntax:

```
public abstract class Shape {
    abstract public void Draw();  // no body, just the method header
}

public class Circle extends Shape {
    public void Draw() {
        // code for Circle's Draw method goes here
    }
}

public class Square extends Shape {
    public void Draw() {
        // code for Square's Draw method goes here
    }
}

public class Rectangle extends Shape {
    public void Draw() {
        // code for Rectangle's Draw method goes here
    }
}
```

Note that if a class includes an abstract method, the class *must* be declared abstract, too (otherwise you get a compile-time error). Also, an abstract class cannot be instantiated (you cannot create an instance of the class itself, only of one of its subclasses). For example:

```
Shape s;           // OK -- just a pointer to a Shape,
                   //      no attempt to create a Shape object
s = new Circle();  // OK -- Circle is not an abstract class
s = new Shape();   // Error!  Can't instantiate an abstract class
```

Interfaces

Some objects have more than one "is-a" relationship. For example, consider designing classes to represent some of the people associated with a university. One way to think of the hierarchical relationship among those people is as shown below:

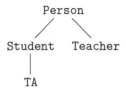

This diagram says that a TA (a teaching assistant) is a student, a student is a person, and a teacher is also a person. However, although a TA is certainly a student, in some ways, a TA is also a teacher (e.g., a TA teaches a class and gets paid). Java does not allow you to make the TA class a subclass of both the Student class and the Teacher class. One solution to this problem is to make TA a subclass of the Student class and to use an *interface* to define what TAs and teachers have in common.

An interface is similar to a class, but it can only contain:

- public, static, final fields (i.e., constants)
- public, abstract methods (i.e., just method headers, no bodies)

Here's an example:

```
public interface Employee {
    void raiseSalary( double d );
    double getSalary();
}
```

Note that both methods are implicitly public and abstract (those keywords can be provided, but are not necessary).

A class can *implement* one or more interfaces (in addition to extending one class). It must provide bodies for all of the methods declared in the interface, or else it must be abstract. For example:

```
public class TA implements Employee extends Student {
    public void raiseSalary( double d ) {
        ⋮ actual code here
    }
    public double getSalary() {
        ⋮ actual code here
    }
}
```

Many classes can implement the same interface (e.g., both the TA class and the Teacher class can implement the Employee interface). Interfaces provide a way to group similar objects. For example, you could write a method with a parameter named emp of type Employee, and then call that method with either a TA or a Teacher object. The compiler would make sure that the method was never called with a non-Employee argument (e.g., a call with a Student argument would cause a compile-time error), and dynamic dispatch (polymorphism) would ensure that code like emp.raiseSalary(2.0) would correctly call the raiseSalary method of the TA or Teacher class, depending on the type of the object actually pointed to by parameter emp.

If you don't use the Employee interface, it would not be possible to write a single method with a parameter that was either a TA or a Teacher, but not a Person or Student.

Generic Classes and Interfaces

A *generic* class or interface is one that is parameterized by one or more types. The type parameters appear at the end of the class or interface name, enclosed in angle brackets. For example:

```
public class ArrayList<E>
```

The type parameters can be used inside the class or interface definition anywhere a "normal" type could be used; for example, as the type of a field, the return type of a method, or the type of a method's parameters. AP CS students are *not* expected to design or implement generic classes or interfaces. However, they are expected to understand how generic classes and interfaces are used. For example, students should understand that an ArrayList that will contain Integers should be declared and initialized as follows:

```
ArrayList<Integer> A = new ArrayList<Integer>();
```

Using generic classes helps avoid the need for class casts and for the runtime checks that go with them, and also eliminates the possibility of a runtime error if the runtime check fails.

For example, suppose that variable A is declared like this

```
ArrayList A;
```

If A is supposed to contain strings, and you want to get the first two characters of the first string, you would have to use a class cast to tell the compiler that the value returned by A.get(0) is a string:

```
((String)A.get(0)).substring(0,2)
```

In this case, there would be a runtime check to make sure that the first item in A is really a string, and there would be a runtime error if it were not a string.

However, if you declare A like this:

```
ArrayList<String> A;
```

then the compiler will ensure that only strings are put into A. This means that there is no need for the class cast in the example code above, there is no need for a runtime check, and no possibility of a runtime error.

Practice Multiple-Choice Questions

1. Consider writing a program to be used by a restaurant to keep track of the items on the menu, which include appetizers, main dishes, and desserts. The restaurant wants to keep track, for every menu item, of the ingredients needed to prepare that item. Some operations will be implemented that apply to all menu items, and there will also be some specialized operations for each of the three different kinds of menu items.

    Which of the following is the best design?

    A. Define one class `MenuItem` with four fields: `Appetizer`, `MainDish`, `Dessert`, and `Ingredients`.

    B. Define three unrelated classes: `Appetizer`, `MainDish`, and `Dessert`, each of which has an `Ingredients` field.

    C. Define a superclass `MenuItem` with three subclasses: `Appetizer`, `MainDish`, and `Dessert`, and with an `Ingredients` field.

    D. Define a superclass `MenuItem` with four subclasses: `Appetizer`, `MainDish`, `Dessert`, and `Ingredients`.

    E. Define four classes: `Appetizer`, `MainDish`, `Dessert`, and `Ingredients`. Make `Ingredients` a subclass of `Dessert`, make `Dessert` a subclass of `MainDish`, and make `MainDish` a subclass of `Appetizer`.

2. Consider the following (incomplete) class definitions:

    ```
    public abstract class Shape {
       public Shape() { ... }

       public abstract void print();
    }

    public class Square extends Shape {
       public Square() { ... }

       public void print() {
          System.out.println("square");
       }
    }
    ```

    Which of the following statements does *not* cause a compile-time error?

    I.   `Shape s = new Square();`
    II. `Shape s = new Shape();`
    III. `Square s = new Shape();`

    A. I only

    B. II only

    C. III only

    D. I and II only

    E. II and III only

Questions 3 and 4 refer to the following (incomplete) class definitions.

```
public class Person {
   public Person() { ... }
   public void print() { System.out.println("person"); }
   public static void printAll( Person[] list ) {
      for (Person p : list) p.print();
   }
}


public class Student extends Person {
   public void print() { System.out.println("student"); }
}
```

3. Consider the following code:

```
ArrayList L = new ArrayList();
Student s;
Person p = new Person();
L.add(p);
statement
```

Which of the following can be used to replace the placeholder *statement* so that the code will cause neither a compile-time nor a runtime error?

A. `p = (Student)(L.get(0));`

B. `p = (Person)(L.get(0));`

C. `s = L.get(0);`

D. `s = (Person)(L.get(0));`

E. `s = (Student)(L.get(0));`

4. Assume that method `printAll` is called with an array of length five, and that none of the five elements of the array is `null`. Which of the following statements best describes what will happen, and why?

A. The word `person` will be printed five times since the type of the array parameter is `Person`.

B. The word `person` will be printed five times since `printAll` is a method of the `Person` class.

C. The word `student` will be printed five times since the `print` method was overridden by the `Student` class.

D. For each of the five objects in the array, either the word `person` or the word `student` will be printed, depending on the type of the object.

E. If the array actually contains objects of type `Person`, then the word `person` will be printed five times; otherwise, a runtime error will occur.

5. Consider the following interface and class definitions:

```
public interface Employee {
   void raiseSalary();
}

public interface Musician {
   void Play();
}

public class Test implements Employee, Musician {
   public void raiseSalary() {
      System.out.println("raising");
   }

   public void Play() {
      System.out.println("playing");
   }
}
```

Which of the following statements about these definitions is true?

A. The code will not compile because class Test tries to implement two interfaces at once.

B. The code will not compile because class Test only implements interfaces; it does not extend any class.

C. The code will not compile because class Test only implements the methods defined in the Employee and Musician interfaces; it does not define any new methods.

D. The code will compile; however, if class Test did not include a definition of the Play method, the code would not compile.

E. The code will compile; furthermore, even if class Test did not include a definition of the Play method, the code would compile.

Answers to Multiple-Choice Questions

1. C
2. A
3. B
4. D
5. D

2.3   Arrays of Objects

The example arrays in Chapter 1 were all arrays of int or String. However, an array can contain any type, including objects other than strings, and it is important to understand how to use such arrays: how to create objects and put them into an array, how to access the objects in an array, how to call the methods of those objects, and how to access the fields of those objects (when appropriate). It is also important to understand the difference between initializing an array of objects and initializing the objects themselves.

To illustrate these ideas, we will use the (incomplete) Date and Person classes shown below.

```java
public class Date {
    private int month;
    private int day;
    private int year;

    public Date(int aMonth, int aDay, int aYear) {
        month = aMonth;
        day = aDay;
        year = aYear;
    }

    // return a negative integer, zero, or a positive integer
    // depending on whether this date is earlier than, the same as,
    // or later than other
    public int compareTo(Object other) {
        : code not shown
    }
}

public class Person {
    private String firstName;
    private String lastName;
    private Date birthday;
    private Person[] siblings;

    public Person(String first, String last, Date bDay) {
        firstName = first;
        lastName = last;
        birthday = bDay;
        siblings = null;
    }
```

```
    public void setSiblings(Person[] sibs) {
        siblings = sibs;
    }

    public String getFirstName() {
        return firstName;
    }

    public Person oldestSib() {
    // precondition: siblings.length > 0 and
    //               siblings contains no nulls
    // postcondition: returns the oldest sibling
        int index = 0;
        Date sibDate = siblings[index].birthday;
        for (int k=1; k<siblings.length; k++) {
            ⋮ missing code
        }
        return siblings[index];
    }
}
```

First, let's consider how to create an array to hold three people. We could start by declaring and initializing an array variable as follows:

```
Person[] personList;
personList = new Person[3];
```

It is important to realize that while this statement initializes the personList array, there are not yet any people in the array (instead, each item in the array is null). In order to fill the array with people, we must use new to create the people, just as we used new above to create the array itself. To illustrate this more clearly, the declaration and initialization of the array are repeated on the next page, followed by code that fills in the first two elements of the array. Each line of code is illustrated to show what happens at runtime.

Now let's consider how to access and use the people in an array by filling in the missing code in the oldestSib method. The code needs to compare the birthday in variable sibDate with the birthday of the kth person in the siblings array; if the birthday of the person in the array is earlier, the index and sibDate variables need to be updated. (Note that since the oldestSib method is part of the Person class, this code can access the private fields of the people in the array.) There are different ways to write the missing code: We could first get the kth person from the siblings array, then get that person's birthday, and then check whether the birthday comes

```
Person[] personList;
```

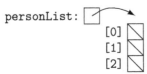

```
personList = new Person[3];
```

personList:

```
personList[0] = new Person("Sandy", "Smith", new Date(6, 28, 1995));
```

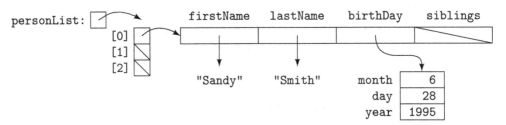

```
personList[1] = new Person("Iris", "Wong", new Date(10, 12, 1990));
```

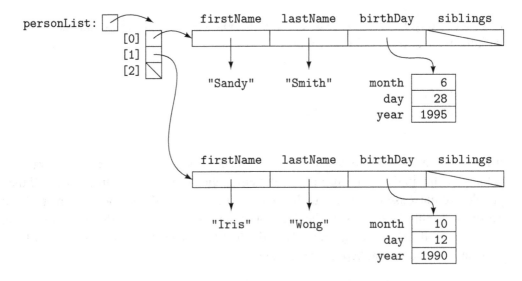

before `sibDate` (updating `index` and `sibDate` if it does). In that case, the *for-loop* would be as shown below (remember that the method call `d.compareTo(sibDate)` returns a negative integer if `d` is earlier than `sibDate`, zero if the two dates are the same, and a positive integer if `d` is later than `sibDate`):

```
for (int k=1; k<siblings.length; k++) {
    Person p = siblings[k];
    Date d = p.birthday;
    if (d.compareTo(sibDate) < 0) {
        index = k;
        sibDate = d;
    }
}
```

We could also compare the two dates using a single expression in the *if* statement like this:

```
for (int k=1; k<siblings.length; k++) {
    if (siblings[k].birthday.compareTo(sibDate) < 0) {
        index = k;
        sibDate = siblings[k].birthday;
    }
}
```

To understand this version of the *if* statement, it helps to think about the types of the subexpressions of siblings[k].birthday.compareTo(sibDate). The type of siblings[k] is Person, and the type of siblings[k].birthday is Date (the birthday of the kth person in the array, counting from zero). The whole expression, siblings[k].birthday.compareTo(sibDate), calls the compareTo method of the kth person's birthday, so its type is the result type of compareTo, which is an int. Therefore, it is correct to see if that result is less than zero (i.e., does the kth person's birthday come before sibDate).

Now let's consider how to write code that manipulates an array of people but is *not* part of the Person class, so the code cannot access the fields of the Person class directly. For example, suppose we have an array of people (in a variable named personList) and a first name (in a variable named firstName), and we want to remove from the array all people who have that first name; that is, we want to end up with a *smaller* array that only includes people with a different first name. To accomplish this, we could do the following:

- Go through the array, counting how many people have the given first name.
- If the count is zero, then do nothing further. Otherwise, create a new array with just enough space for the people who do not have the given first name; go through the personList array again, and copy the people who don't have the given first name into the new array. Then set personList to point to the new array.

Here's one way to write the code; this time we'll use a for-each loop to iterate over all of the people in the array.

```
int counter = 0;

// count how many people in personList have firstName
for (Person p : personList) {
    String oneName = p.getFirstName();
    if (oneName.equals(firstName)) {
        counter++;
    }
}
```

```
if (counter != 0) {
   // create a new array, fill it with the people who do not
   // have firstName, and set personList to point to the new array
   Person[] newList = new Person[personList.length - counter];
   int newIndex = 0;
   for (Person p : personList) {
      String oneName = p.getFirstName();
      if (! oneName.equals(firstName)) {
         newList[newIndex] = p;
         newIndex++;
      }
   }
   personList = newList;
}
```

We could also write the comparison of person p's name with the given name as a single expression, without using local variable oneName:

```
if (p.getFirstName().equals(firstName)) {
   counter++;
}
```

In this version of the code, the *if* condition has two method calls: first p's getFirstName method is called, returning a String; then that String's equals method is called to see if it matches firstName. Some people find the first version easier to understand, but both versions of the code are correct, and it would be fine to use either version for a free-response question on the AP CS exam.

Practice Multiple-Choice Questions

Questions 1–4 refer to the following Time class.

```
public class Time {
// a Time represents the time needed to do some task;
// e.g., 4 hours and 20 minutes, or 32 hours and 3 minutes

   private int hours;   // 0 <= hours
   private int minutes; // 0 <= minutes <= 59

   public Time(int hrs, int mins) {
      hours = hrs;
      minutes = mins;
   }
   public int getHours() { return hours; }
   public int getMinutes() { return minutes; }
   public void setHours(int hrs) { hours = hrs; }
   public void setMinutes(int mins) { minutes = mins;}
}
```

1. Consider the following instance variable and method (*not* part of the Time class).

    ```
    private Time[] myTimes;

    public Time longestTime() {
    // precondition: myTimes.length > 0 and
    //                myTimes contains no nulls
    // postcondition: returns the longest Time in myTimes
       Time t = myTimes[0];
       for (int k=1; k<myTimes.length; k++) {
          if (missing condition) {
             t = myTimes[k];
          }
       }
       return t;
    }
    ```

    Which of the following code segments could be used to replace *missing condition* so that
    longestTime works as specified by its pre- and postconditions?

    A. myTimes[k].hours > t.hours

    B. myTimes[k].getHours() > t.hours

    C. myTimes[k].getHours() > t.getHours()

    D. (myTimes[k].getHours() > t.getHours()) ||
       (myTimes[k].getMinutes() > t.getMinutes())

    E. (myTimes[k].getHours() > t.getHours()) ||
          ((myTimes[k].getHours() == t.getHours()) &&
            (myTimes[k].getMinutes() > t.getMinutes()))

2. Assume that variable `timeList` has been declared to be an array of `Time`s as follows:

```
Time[] timeList;
```

Which of the following code segments correctly initializes the array to contain ten `Time`s, each representing the time "3 hours and 20 minutes"?

```
I.   timeList = new Time[10];
II.  timeList = new Time[10];
     for (int k=0; k<10; k++) {
        timeList[k].setHours(3);
        timeList[k].setMinutes(20);
     }
III. timeList = new Time[10];
     for (int k=0; k<10; k++) {
        timeList[k] = new Time(3, 20);
     }
```

A. I only

B. II only

C. III only

D. II and III only

E. I, II, and III

3. Consider the following code segment:

```
Time[] myTimes = new Time[N];
for (int k=0; k<myTimes.length; k+=2) {
   System.out.println(myTimes[k].getHours());
}
```

Assume that `N` is a positive `int`. Which of the following is true?

A. The code will not compile because the *for-loop* does not access all of the items in the array.

B. The code will compile, but there will be a `NullPointerException` when it executes.

C. The code will compile, but there will be an `IndexOutOfBoundsException` when it executes.

D. The code will compile and execute without error; it will print the values of the hours in `myTimes[0]`, `myTimes[2]`, `myTimes[4]`, and so on.

E. The code will compile and execute without error; it will print the values of the hours in `myTimes[2]`, `myTimes[4]`, and so on.

4. Consider the following code segment:

```
Time[] myTimes = new Time[3];
Time t = new Time(1, 15);
myTimes[0] = t;
myTimes[1] = t;
myTimes[2] = t;
myTimes[1].setMinutes(43);
for (int k=0; k<3; k++) {
    System.out.print(myTimes[k].getMinutes() + " ");
}
```

What happens when this code executes?

A. There is a `NullPointerException`.

B. There is an `IndexOutOfBoundsException`.

C. There is no exception; 15 15 15 is printed.

D. There is no exception; 15 43 15 is printed.

E. There is no exception; 43 43 43 is printed.

5. Assume that a class XX has been defined that includes a definition of the `equals` method. Consider the following declarations and incomplete method:

```
private XX[] A1;
private XX[] A2;

public boolean arraysEq() {
// precondition: A1.length > 0 and A2.length > 0 and
//               neither A1 nor A2 contains a null
// postcondition: returns true iff A1 and A2 contain
//                the same objects in the same order
    if (A1.length != A2.length) return false;
      ⋮ missing code
}
```

Which of the following code segments could be used to replace *missing code* so that `arraysEq` works as specified by its pre- and postconditions?

A.
```
for (int k=0; k<A1.length; k++) {
    if (! A1[k].equals(A2[k])) return false;
}
return true;
```

B.
```
for (int k=0; k<A1.length; k++) {
    if (! A1[k] == A2[k]) return false;
}
return true;
```

C. `return (A1.equals(A2));`

D. `return (A1 == A2);`

E. `return true;`

Answers to Multiple-Choice Questions

1. E
2. C
3. B
4. E
5. A

3
Design and Analysis of Data Structures and Algorithms

Designing good data structures and algorithms is a very important part of programming. Data structure design includes defining the set of operations that will be available to the users of the data structure (the *interface*), as well as designing the way the data will actually be stored (the *implementation*). A data structure should be designed with the following goals in mind:

- The code that uses the data structure should be easy to understand.
- The data structure should be easy to modify (e.g., by adding new operations).
- The code that implements the data structure should be reasonably efficient.

Students should be able to compare several proposed ways to define data structures, explaining the advantages and disadvantages of each. Students should also be able to compare the space and time requirements of different data structure and algorithm designs.

Practice Multiple-Choice Questions

Questions 1 and 2 refer to the following information:

A farmer has N barns. Each barn contains cows, sheep, or pigs. The farmer wants a data structure to record the following information for each barn:

- The day of the year the animals in the barn were purchased (a number in the range 1 to 365).
- The kind of animals in the barn.
- The number of animals in the barn.

The farmer plans to define a class named `Barn` to hold information about one barn, and to use an array of `Barn`s of length N to store information about each of the N barns.

The farmer is considering two possible ways to define the fields of the `Barn` class:

Definition 1: Use three fields of type `int`, `String`, and `int` to hold the three pieces of information for each barn.

Definition 2: Use one field that is an `int` array of length three. The three elements of the array will hold the three pieces of information for each barn.

1. Which of the following is the best reason for preferring definition 1 over definition 2?

    A. Definition 2 will not work, since the kind of animal in the barn cannot be represented using an integer.

    B. Less space will be used by definition 1 than by definition 2.

    C. Less time will be needed to determine the number of animals in a given barn using definition 1 than using definition 2.

    D. Using three named fields, rather than a single array, makes it clearer how the data are to be stored in each instance of a `Barn`.

    E. Since the information about all N barns is to be stored in an array, it is better not to use an array in the definition of the `Barn` class.

2. Assume that definition 1 has been chosen. Which of the following is a true statement about printing all of the information about the kth barn?

    A. It can be done equally efficiently for all values of k between 0 and $N - 1$.

    B. The time required will be proportional to k.

    C. The time required will be proportional to N.

    D. The time required will be proportional to $k + N$.

    E. The time required will be proportional to $k * N$.

Questions 3 and 4 refer to the following information:

A teacher needs a data structure to store information about student absences each day of the 80-day semester. There are N students in the class. Two different designs are being considered.

Design 1: A one-dimensional array with 80 elements. Each element of the array is an `ArrayList` of N strings. Each string is either "absent" or "present."

Design 2: A two-dimensional array with 80 rows and N columns. Each element of the array contains a boolean value (`true` or `false`).

Assume that more space is required to store a string than to store a boolean value.

3. Which of the following statements about the space requirements of the two designs is true?

    A. Design 1 will require more space than design 2.

    B. Design 2 will require more space than design 1.

    C. Designs 1 and 2 will require the same amount of space.

    D. Which design will require more space depends on how many students are actually absent during the semester.

    E. Which design will require more space depends on the value of N.

4. Assume that design 2 is chosen and that the following operation is implemented as efficiently as possible.

> Given a student number j (between 1 and N) and a day number k (between 1 and 80), look in the data structure to see whether student j was absent on day k.

Which of the following statements is true?

A. The time required to perform the operation is proportional to the size of the array.

B. The time required to perform the operation is proportional to the number of students absent on the given day.

C. The time required to perform the operation is proportional to the total number of students.

D. The time required to perform the operation is proportional to the number of days in the semester.

E. The time required to perform the operation is independent of the number of students absent on the given day, the total number of students, and the number of days in the semester.

5. Consider the following code segment:

```
int N = some positive integer value;
for (int k=1; k<=N; k++) {
    for (int j=1; j<=N; j++) {
        System.out.print("*");
    }
}
```

How many stars are printed when this code segment executes?

A. $N/2$
B. N
C. $N*2$
D. $N*N$
E. $N*N*N$

Answers to Multiple-Choice Questions

1. D
2. A
3. A
4. E
5. D

4

Lists

Students should be familiar with the `java.util.ArrayList<E>` class and the `java.util.List<E>` interface. Those topics are discussed in this chapter.

4.1 The `java.util.ArrayList<E>` Class

An `ArrayList` is a "built-in" class that gives you a way to store an ordered list of objects. Note that "ordered" doesn't mean that the objects are in *sorted* order, it just means that each object has a *position* in the list, starting with position zero. `ArrayList` is a *generic* class (see Chapter 2). It is parameterized by the type of the objects stored in the list. So, for example, if you want a list of strings, you would use a declaration like this:

```
ArrayList<String> myList;
```

If instead you used

```
ArrayList myList;
```

you could store any kind of `Object` in the list, but you would have to use a class cast to get strings out of the list.

Students should be familiar with the `ArrayList` methods that allow you to add an object (to the end of the list or at a particular position in the list), get the object at a particular position, remove an object from a particular position (returning the removed object), replace the object at a particular position with another one (returning the replaced object), and see how many objects are currently in the list. Here are the `ArrayList<E>` methods:

Method	Explanation
`boolean add(E x)`	Adds x to the end of this list and returns `true`.
`void add(int n, E x)`	If index n is out of bounds (n < 0 or n > `size()`), throws an `IndexOutOfBoundsException`. Otherwise, moves the elements in positions n (counting from zero) to the end of this list over one place to the right to make room for new element x, then inserts x at position n in this list.

`E get(int n)`	If index n is out of bounds (`n < 0` or `n >= size()`), throws an `IndexOutOfBoundsException`. Otherwise, returns the element at position n (counting from zero) in this list.
`E remove(int n)`	If index n is out of bounds (`n < 0` or `n >= size()`), throws an `IndexOutOfBoundsException`. Otherwise, removes the element at position n (counting from zero) in this list, then shifts the remaining elements over one place to the left to fill in the gap. Returns the removed element.
`E set(int n, Object x)`	If index n is out of bounds (`n < 0` or `n >= size()`), throws an `IndexOutOfBoundsException`. Otherwise, replaces the element at position n (counting from zero) in this list with x and returns the replaced element.
`int size()`	Returns the number of elements in this list.

The main advantage of an `ArrayList` compared to a plain array is that, whereas the size of an array is fixed when it is created (e.g., `int[] A = new int[10]` creates an array of integers of size 10, and you cannot store more than 10 integers in that array), the size of an `ArrayList` can change: The size increases by one each time a new item is added (using either version of the add method), and the size decreases by one each time an item is removed (using the `remove` method).

One disadvantage of an `ArrayList` compared to a plain array is that, whereas you can create an array of any size, and then you can fill in any element in that array, a new `ArrayList` always has size zero, and you can never add an object at a position greater than the size. For example, the following code is fine:

```
Object[] obList = new obList[10];
obList[5] = "hello";
```

but this code will cause a runtime exception:

```
ArrayList<String> obList = new ArrayList<String>();
obList.add(5, "hello");        // error! can only add at position 0
```

Below is code that uses an `ArrayList` to create a list of the integers from 1 to 10, and to print them in order.

```
ArrayList<Integer> list = new ArrayList<Integer>();
for (int k=1; k<=10; k++) {
    list.add(new Integer(k));
}
for (Integer tmp : list) {
    System.out.println(tmp.intValue());
}
```

An ArrayList is implemented using an array. This means, for example, that adding an item to the end of an ArrayList of length N is very efficient (does not depend on N), but adding or removing an item at position k requires moving $N-k$ items (all of the items to the right of the one that was added or removed), so the time required is proportional to $N-k$. Getting or replacing any item from an ArrayList is also very efficient, because the get and set methods require using just one indexing operation in the array used to implement the ArrayList (no items need to be moved).

To further demonstrate how to use an ArrayList, we'll use the Date and Person classes defined in Chapter 2, but we'll change the siblings field to be an ArrayList instead of an array. This requires changing method oldestSib, too. The new field declaration and the code for that method are given below, with line numbers included for reference.

```
1  private ArrayList<Person> siblings;

2  public Person oldestSib() {
3  // precondition: siblings.size() > 0 and
4  //                siblings contains no nulls
5  // postcondition: returns the oldest sibling
6     int index = 0;
7     Date sibDate = siblings.get(index).birthday;
8     for (int k=1; k<siblings.size(); k++) {
9        Person p = siblings.get(k);
10       Date d = p.birthday;
11       if (d.compareTo(sibDate) < 0) {
12          index = k;
13          sibDate = d;
14       }
15    }
16    return siblings.get(index);
17 }
```

Note that there are several differences between this version of the oldestSib method and the one that uses an array of people:

- On lines 7, 9, and 16, we use the ArrayList's get method to get a person from the list, while in the previous version we used indexing.
- On line 8, we use the ArrayList's size method to find out how many people are in the list, while in the previous version we used the array's length field.

Now let's consider the code we'd need to create either an *array* or an ArrayList containing N people (where N is some positive integer). We'll assume that method createPerson creates and returns one Person, using information from a file.

Array Version	**ArrayList Version**

```
Person[] personList;
personList = new Person[N];
for (int k=0; k<N; k++) {
    Person p = createPerson();
    personList[k] = p;
}
```

```
ArrayList<Person> personList;
personList = new ArrayList<Person>();
for (int k=0; k<N; k++) {
    Person p = createPerson();
    personList.add(p);
}
```

In the two versions, the first two lines (the declaration and initialization of variable `personList`) and the last lines (the code that adds a new person to the list) are different.

In the `ArrayList` version of the code given above, we used the add method that has just one `Object` parameter, and that adds that object to the end of the list. We could also have used the version that has two parameters, the index at which to add and the object to be added:

```
personList.add(k, p);
```

In either case, the `ArrayList` is filled in from left to right; that is, the first person gets added at position zero, the second person at position one, and so on. Let's think about what we'd have to do to fill in an array or an `ArrayList` from right to left. For an array, we could simply let our *for-loop* index run from N–1 down to 0 as follows:

```
Person[] personList = new Person[N];
for (int k=N-1; k>=0; k--) {
    Person p = createPerson();
    personList[k] = p;
}
```

However, if we tried to do something similar with an `ArrayList`, we'd get a runtime error:

```
ArrayList<Person> personList = new ArrayList<Person>();
for (int k=N-1; k>=0; k--) {
    Person p = createPerson();
    personList.add(k, p);  // causes a runtime error!
}
```

The problem is that you can't call an `ArrayList`'s add method with an index greater than its size; that is, you can only add a new item at the end of the list or at a position in the list that already contains an item (in which case that item and all of the items to its right are moved over one place to make room for the new item).

To fill in an `ArrayList` from right to left, we need to add each new person to the *front* of the `ArrayList` (i.e., add it at position zero) like this:

```
ArrayList<Person> personList = new ArrayList<Person>();
for (int k=0; k<N; k++) {
    Person p = createPerson();
    personList.add(0, p);
}
```

Is it equally efficient to store the N people in an array or in an ArrayList? If we add them left-to-right, then the answer is yes, because putting a person anywhere in an array takes the same amount of time as adding a person to the end of an ArrayList; it is independent of the size of the array or of the list. However, if we add the people right-to-left, then the answer is no. Adding each of them to the array is still independent of the size of the array, so initializing the whole array of N people takes time proportional to N. However, each call to the ArrayList's add method takes time proportional to the current size of the list, and so the total time to create the ArrayList is proportional to N^2.

Finally, let's rewrite the code that removes from a list all of the people with a given first name. Since we can use the ArrayList's remove method (which changes the size of the list), this code is easier to write when variable personList is an ArrayList instead of an array. It is no longer necessary to count the number of people with the given first name, nor to create a new ArrayList; instead, we simply call the ArrayList's remove method each time we find a person with the given first name:

```
int k = 0;
while (k<personList.size()) {
    Person p = personList.get(k);
    String oneName = p.getFirstName();
    if (oneName.equals(firstName)) {
        personList.remove(k);
    } else {
        k++;
    }
}
```

Note that when the kth person in the list has the given first name we do *not* increment k. This is because calling the remove method causes a new person to move into the kth position, and we need to check whether that person needs to be removed from the list, too. For example, if the first names of the people in the list are:

```
Deborah   Sarah   Sarah   Mary   Sarah
```

and the given name is Sarah, then the first call to remove will happen when k is 1. That will change the list so that the first names of the remaining people are:

```
Deborah   Sarah   Mary   Sarah
```

and k will still be 1. If we increment k to 2, the next first name we'll check will be Mary; that is, we'll fail to check the first name of the second Sarah in the (original) list. Clearly, that is not correct, so we should only increment k when the first name of the kth person does *not* match firstName.

Although this code is simpler than the code we wrote when personList was an array, there is a disadvantage in terms of efficiency. The array version of the code required going through the personList array twice: once to count the number of people with the given first name, and once to copy those people to the new array. Therefore, the time required to execute the array version of the code will be proportional to the size of the original array. The ArrayList version of the code only goes through the ArrayList once, but each time the remove method is called, all of the items to the right of the one being removed have to be moved over one position in the list. This means that, in the worst case, the time for the `ArrayList` version will be proportional to N^2, where N is the original size of the list.

4.2 The `java.util.List<E>` Interface

The `java.util.ArrayList<E>` class implements the `java.util.List<E>` interface. That interface includes the following methods:

Method	Explanation
`boolean add(E x)`	Adds x to the end of this list and returns `true`.
`void add(int n, E x)`	If index n is out of bounds (n < 0 or n > size()), throws an Index OutOfBoundsException. Otherwise, adds x to this list in position n (counting from zero), after moving the elements in positions n and higher one place to the right (adding 1 to their indexes).
`E get(int n)`	If index n is out of bounds (n < 0 or n >= size()), throws an Index OutOfBoundsException. Otherwise, returns the element at position n (counting from zero) in this list.
`E set(int n, E x)`	If index n is out of bounds (n < 0 or n >= size()), throws an Index OutOfBoundsException. Otherwise, replaces the element at position n (counting from zero) in this list with x and returns the object that was previously at position n.
`E remove(int n)`	If index n is out of bounds (n < 0 or n >= size()), throws an Index OutOfBoundsException. Otherwise, removes the element at position n (counting from zero) from this list, moving the elements at positions n+1 and higher one place to the left (subtracting 1 from their indices) and returns the element that was removed.
`int size()`	Returns the number of elements in this list.

If you want to implement an operation on lists that would use the same code whether that list is an `ArrayList` or some other kind of list, then it makes sense to define that operation using a method with a `List` parameter, instead of writing multiple copies, each with a particular kind of list as its parameter. Examples of operations that you might want to use in this way include printing the list and removing all instances of a particular object from the list. Below are methods that implement those two operations. The first example uses a `for-each` loop (since it iterates through the whole list without changing it), and the second example uses a while loop (since it may remove items from the list, and to do that it needs the index of the item being removed).

```
// Example 1: Print the items in a list
public static void printList(List<Object> L) {
// precondition: L is not null
   for (Object item : L) {
      System.out.println( item );
   }
}
```

```
// Example 2: Remove all instances of item from list L
public static void removeFromList(List<Object> L, Object ob) {
// precondition: neither ob nor L is null
// postcondition: all instances of ob have been removed from L
    int pos = 0;
    while (pos < L.size()) {
        if (ob.equals(L.get(pos))) L.remove(pos);
        else pos++;
    }
}
```

Practice Multiple-Choice Questions

1. Assume that variable myList is an ArrayList containing at least two objects. Which of the following code segments moves the first object in the list to the end of the list?

   A. `myList.add(myList.get(0));`

   B. `myList.add(myList.remove(0));`

   C. `myList.add(0, myList.remove(0));`

   D. `myList.add(myList.size(), myList.get(0));`

   E. `myList.add(myList.remove(myList.size()-1));`

2. Consider the following code segment:

   ```
   ArrayList<Integer> L = new ArrayList<Integer>();
   for (int k=0; k<9; k++) {
      L.add(new Integer(k));
   }
   for (int k=0; k<5; k++) {
      Object tmp = L.get(k);
      L.set(k, L.get(8-k));
      L.set(8-k, tmp);
   }
   for (int k=0; k<9; k++) {
      System.out.print(L.get(k) + " ");
   }
   ```

   What is printed when this code executes?

   A. 0 1 2 3 4 5 6 7 8

   B. 8 7 6 5 4 3 2 1 0

   C. 0 1 2 3 4 3 2 1 0

   D. 0 0 0 0 0 0 0 0 0

   E. 8 8 8 8 8 8 8 8 8

3. Assume that variable L is an `ArrayList` and that the method call `L.size()` returns 10. Which of the following method calls does *not* cause a runtime error?

   A. `L.add(10, "hello")`

   B. `L.add(20, "hello")`

   C. `L.get(10)`

   D. `L.set(10, "hello")`

   E. `L.remove(10)`

4. Which of the following statements will compile without error?

   I.   `ArrayList<String> L = new List<String>();`
   II. `ArrayList<String> L = new ArrayList<String>();`
   III. `List<String> L = new ArrayList<String>();`

   A. I only

   B. II only

   C. III only

   D. I and II

   E. II and III

5. Assume that the type of variable `strList` is `ArrayList<String>`. Consider the following two code segments, both of which are intended to add an exclamation point to the end of each string in the list.

Segment 1	Segment 2
```for (int k=0; k<strList.size(); k++) { Str tmp = strList.remove(k); strList.add(k, tmp + "!"); }```	```for (int k=0; k<strList.size(); k++) { String tmp = strList.get(k); strList.set(k, tmp + "!"); }```

Which of the following statements about these two code segments is true?

   A. Both will work as intended, and they will be equally efficient.

   B. Both will work as intended; segment 1 will be more efficient than segment 2.

   C. Both will work as intended; segment 2 will be more efficient than segment 1.

   D. Only segment 1 will work as intended.

   E. Only segment 2 will work as intended.

Answers to Multiple-Choice Questions

1. B
2. B
3. A
4. C
5. C

5
Sorting and Searching

5.1 Sorting

Students should be familiar with three standard sorting algorithms: Selection Sort and Insertion Sort (both of which can require time proportional to N^2 to sort a list of N values), and the more efficient Merge Sort. Students should also be able to reason about the efficiency of a new sorting algorithm, given a description of how it works. In the reviews of Selection, Insertion, and Merge Sort given below, it is assumed that the values to be sorted are in an array.

Selection Sort

Selection Sort works by finding the smallest element in the array and swapping it with the value in position zero, then finding the second smallest element and swapping it with the value in position one, and so on. If there are N values to be sorted, Selection Sort will make N passes through the array of values. The first time, it will look at all N values; the second time, it will look at $N - 1$ values; the third time, it will look at $N - 2$ values; and so on. So the time required by Selection Sort is proportional to:

$$N + (N - 1) + (N - 2) + \cdots + 3 + 2 + 1$$

This is proportional to N^2. If the values in the array are already in sorted order, Selection Sort will still make the same passes through the array (although it will not do any swaps). Therefore, the time for Selection Sort is proportional to N^2 regardless of how close to sorted the values are initially.

Insertion Sort

Insertion Sort works by making one pass through the array of values; each time it considers an element, it goes *back* through the array to find the appropriate place for that element. In the worst case (when the array of values is initially in *reverse* sorted order), it will have to go all the way back to the beginning of the array every time it considers an element. In that case, for the first element it will look at zero previous values; for the second element, it will look at one previous value; for the third element, it will look at two previous values; and so on. So the time required by Insertion Sort in this case is proportional to:

$$0 + 1 + 2 + \cdots + (N - 2) + (N - 1)$$

Again, this is proportional to N^2.

However, in the best case (when the array of values is already in sorted order), Insertion Sort will only look at one previous value each time it moves on to the next element. In this case, it will only require time proportional to N.

Merge Sort

Merge Sort works by recursively sorting the two halves of the given array into some auxiliary data structures (e.g., two other arrays, each half the size of the original array) and then merging the sorted values back into the original array. (The recursion ends when there is just one value to be sorted.) For example, assume that the array initially contains the following eight values:

    4   6   7   0   3   9   3   6

The first recursive call would sort the left half of the array, producing the following sorted array (of size four):

    0   4   6   7

And the second recursive call would produce the following sorted array:

    3   3   6   9

The two sorted arrays would be merged to produce the following final array:

    0   3   3   4   6   6   7   9

Students should understand that Merge Sort is always more efficient than Selection Sort and usually more efficient than Insertion Sort (except when the array is already sorted or is close to being sorted). However, a disadvantage of Merge Sort is that it requires more space than the other sorting algorithms, because of the auxiliary data structures that it uses.

5.2   Searching

Students should understand how to search for a given value in an array using sequential or binary search. The two searching techniques are reviewed below.

Sequential Search

A *sequential search* simply involves looking at each item in the array in turn until either the value being searched for is found or it can be determined that the value is not in the array. If the array is unsorted, then it is necessary to keep searching as long as the value is not found. However, if the array is sorted, it may be possible to quit searching without examining all of the elements in the array. If the array is sorted from low to high, the search can stop as soon as the current array value is greater than the value being searched for.

In the worst case, a sequential search will require looking at the whole array, so the time required to search an array of size N is proportional to N.

Binary Search

If the array is sorted, a *binary search* can be performed and is usually more efficient than a sequential search. A binary search first looks at the middle element, *m*. If *m* matches the value being searched for, the search is finished. Otherwise, if *m* is greater than the value being searched for, we know that if the value being searched for is in the array at all, it must be to the left of *m* in the array. A new binary search is done on the half of the array to the left of *m*. Similarly, if *m* is less than the value being searched for, we know that if the value being searched for is in the array at all, it must be to the right of *m* in the array. A new binary search is done on the half of the array to the right of *m*. If the value being searched for is not in the array, a new binary search will eventually be done on a portion of the array of size zero. At that point, the search will end (knowing that the value being searched for was not in the original array).

Binary search is proportional to the log (base 2)* of the size of the array.

Practice Multiple-Choice Questions

1. Consider searching for a given value in an array. Which of the following must be true in order to use binary search?

    I.   The values in the array must be integers.
    II. The values in the array must be in sorted order.
    III. The array must not contain any duplicate values.

    A. I only

    B. II only

    C. I and II only

    D. II and III only

    E. I, II, and III

2. Consider searching for a given value in a sorted array. Under which of the following circumstances will sequential search be *faster* than binary search?

    A. The value is not in the array.

    B. The value is in the first element of the array.

    C. The value is in the last element of the array.

    D. The value is in the middle element of the array.

    E. Sequential search will never be faster than binary search.

---

* The log base 2 of *N* is the number of doublings it takes to get *N*, starting with 1. For example, the log of 2 is 1, because only one doubling is required: one times two equals two. The log of 8 is 3, because three doublings are required: one times two equals two, two times two equals four, and four times two equals eight.

Questions 3 and 4 refer to the following code segment (line numbers are included for reference). Assume that variable A is an array of ints of length N.

```
1  for (int k=0; k<N; k++) {
2     for (int j=k+1; j<N; j++) {
3        if (A[j] < A[k]) {
4           swap(A, j, k);
5        }
6        System.out.println(k);
7     }
8  }
```

3. Assume that swap correctly swaps the jth and k^{th} values in array A. Which of the following assertions is true every time line 6 is executed?

   A. The values in array A are sorted from low to high.

   B. The values in A[k] through A[N] are sorted from low to high.

   C. The values in A[k] through A[N] are sorted from high to low.

   D. The values in A[0] through A[k] are sorted from low to high.

   E. The values in A[0] through A[k] are sorted from high to low.

4. Consider comparing this code to the code for Selection Sort, Insertion Sort, and Merge Sort. Which of the following statements about this comparison is true?

   A. The way the code works is most similar to Merge Sort, and it is as efficient as Merge Sort.

   B. The way the code works is most similar to Merge Sort, but it is less efficient than Merge Sort.

   C. The way the code works is most similar to Insertion Sort, and it is as efficient as Insertion Sort both when the array is already in sorted order and when it is not already in sorted order.

   D. The way the code works is most similar to Insertion Sort, but it is less efficient than Insertion Sort when the array is already in sorted order.

   E. The way the code works is most similar to Selection Sort, and it is as efficient as Selection Sort.

5. Consider searching for a given value in an unsorted array. Which of the following will be the most efficient?

   A. Use sequential search.

   B. Sort the array using *Selection Sort*, then use binary search.

   C. Sort the array using *Merge Sort*, then use binary search.

   D. Copy the values into an ArrayList, then use a while-loop and the get method to look for the value.

   E. Copy the values into an ArrayList, then use a for-each loop to look for the value.

Answers to Multiple-Choice Questions

1. B
2. B
3. D
4. E
5. A

6

AP Computer Science Standard Interfaces and Classes

The AP CS exam will make use of some of the interfaces and classes defined in the packages `java.lang` and `java.util`. These interfaces and classes, and the constructors, methods, and fields that may be tested on the AP CS exam are summarized briefly below. Some of them were discussed in more detail in earlier chapters. A "quick reference" guide that summarizes the AP interfaces and classes (possibly containing just the names of the classes and interfaces, and the signatures of the constructors and methods, with no explanations) will be provided as part of the AP CS exam.

6.1 Interface and Classes from the `java.lang` Package

The `java.lang.Object` Class

As discussed in Chapter 1, objects are the basic building blocks of object-oriented programs. The AP CS Java subset includes the following `Object` methods.

The Object Class

`boolean equals(Object other)`	Returns `true` if this `Object` is the same as `other`; otherwise, returns `false`. (Note that the default version returns `true` if and only if the `==` operator returns `true`; that is, if and only if this `Object` points to the same chunk of memory as `other`.)
`String toString()`	Returns a string representation of this `Object`.

Remember that every class is a subclass of `Object`, so every class inherits the `equals` and `toString` methods of the `Object` class. However, it is often a good idea to redefine these methods when you define a new class so that you get more suitable versions.

For example, consider the following (partial) definition of the Person class:

```
public class Person {
  /*** fields ***/
    private String name;
    private String address;

  /*** constructor ***/
    public Person(String initName, String initAddress) {
      name = initName;
      address = initAddress;
    }

  /*** methods ***/
      ⋮

}
```

Now consider the following code segment:

```
Person p1 = new Person("Chris Smith", "123 Willow St");
Person p2 = new Person("Chris Smith", "123 Willow St");
if (p1.equals(p2)) System.out.println("equal");
else System.out.println("not equal");
```

If the Person class does not redefine the default equals method (inherited from the Object class), "not equal" will be printed, because p1 and p2 point to different chunks of storage. If we want two People objects with the same name and the same address to be considered equal, we must include a new definition of the equals method in the Person class:

```
public boolean equals(Person p) {
    return (name.equals(p.name) && address.equals(p.address));
}
```

The java.lang.Double **and** java.lang.Integer **Classes**

Each Double represents a double value, and each Integer represents an int value. The AP CS Java subset includes the following Double and Integer methods and static fields.

The Double **Class**	
Double(double d)	Constructs a new Double that represents d.
double doubleValue()	Returns the double represented by this Double.
boolean equals(Object other)	Returns true if other is a Double and has the same value; otherwise, returns false.

The `Integer` Class

`Integer(int k)`	Constructs a new `Integer` that represents k.
`int intValue()`	Returns the `int` represented by this `Integer`.
`boolean equals(Object other)`	Returns `true` if `other` is an `Integer` and has the same value; otherwise, returns `false`.
`Integer.MIN_VALUE`	The smallest value an `int` can have.
`Integer.MAX_VALUE`	The largest value an `int` can have.

The `Double` and `Integer` classes are provided so that you can use objects that represent ints and doubles. For example, you might want to create a list of integer values using the `ArrayList` class. Since an `ArrayList` can only store objects, not primitive values, you would create an `Integer` for each integer value that you wanted to store, and add that `Integer` to the `ArrayList`. To get the (plain) integer values back, you would use the `Integer`'s `intValue` method.

Below is code that uses an `ArrayList<Double>` called `dblList` that contains nonnegative Doubles. It creates a new `ArrayList<Integer>` called `intList` that contains the same values rounded to the nearest integer.

```
// precondition: dblList is an ArrayList<Double> of non-null,
//                non-negative Doubles
// postcondition: creates ArrayList<Integer> intList containing the
//                corresponding integer values
ArrayList<Integer> intList = new ArrayList<Integer>();
for (int k=0; k<dblList.size(); k++) {
    Double dbl = dblList.get(k);
    intList.add(new Integer((int)(dbl.doubleValue() + .5)));
}
```

The `java.lang.Math` Class

The `Math` class provides a number of standard mathematical functions. The AP CS Java subset includes the following `Math` methods.

The `Math` Class

`static int abs(int x)`	Returns the absolute value of `int` x.
`static double abs(double x)`	Returns the absolute value of `double` x.
`static double pow(double base, double exponent)`	Returns the value of base raised to the power of exponent.
`static double sqrt(double x)`	Returns the square root of x.
`static double random()`	Returns a double in the range [0.0, 1.0).

Note that all of the Math methods are *static*. This means that when you want to use a Math method, you use the class name followed by a dot followed by the method name, instead of using the name of a Math object followed by a dot followed by the method name. For example, the code segment below includes a use of the abs (absolute value) method of the Math class:

```
double d = -2.0;
double posd = Math.abs(d);  // posd is 2.0
```

The java.lang.String Class

An instance of the String class represents a sequence of zero or more characters. The AP CS Java subset includes the following String methods.

The String Class

int compareTo(Object other)	If other is not a String, throws an exception. Otherwise, returns a negative number if this string comes before other in lexicographic order; returns a positive number if this string comes after other in lexicographic order; returns zero if the two strings are the same.
boolean equals(Object other)	Returns true if other is a String with the same sequence of characters as this one; otherwise, returns false.
int indexOf(String s)	Returns the position of the first occurrence of s in this string, or -1 if s does not occur in this string.
int length()	Returns the number of characters in this string.
String substring(int from, int to)	Returns the substring that starts with the character in position from and ends with the character in position $to - 1$ (counting from zero).
String substring(int from)	Returns the substring that starts with the character in position from (counting from zero) and ends with the last character in the string.

Practice Multiple-Choice Questions

1. Consider the following code segment:

```
String S = "razzle-dazzle"
int k;
k = S.indexOf("z");
while (k != -1) {
   S = S.substring(0, k) + "p" + S.substring(k+1);
   k = S.indexOf("z");
}
System.out.println(S);
```

What is output when this code segment is executed?

A. `rapple-dapple`

B. `rapzle-dazzle`

C. `razzle-dazple`

D. `razzle-dazzle`

E. `ra`

2. Assume that variable A is an array of `Strings` and that variable S is a `String`. Consider the following code segment:

```
for (String oneStr : A) {
   if (oneStr.compareTo(S) < 0) return false;
}
return true;
```

When does this code segment return `true`?

A. When all of the strings in A come before S in lexicographic order

B. When no string in A comes before S in lexicographic order

C. When no string in A comes after S in lexicographic order

D. When some string in A comes before S in lexicographic order

E. When some string in A comes after S in lexicographic order

Questions 3 and 4 concern the following code segment (line numbers are included for use in question 4). Assume that variable S is a String.

```
1 int k = 0;
2 for (int j = S.length()-1; j>=0; j--) {
3    if (! (S.substring(k,k+1).equals(S.substring(j,j+1)))) return false;
4    k++;
5 }
6 return true;
```

3. Which of the following best describes what this code segment does?

  A. Always returns true

  B. Always returns false

  C. Determines whether S is the same forward and backward

  D. Determines whether S contains any duplicate characters

  E. Determines whether the characters in S are in sorted order

4. Consider changing the code segment to make it more efficient. Which of the following changes would accomplish that without changing what the method does?

  A. Change line 2 to:

```
for (int j = S.length()-1; j>=S.length()/2; j--)
```

  B. Change line 2 to:

```
for (int j=0; j<=S.length(); j++)
```

  C. Change line 3 to:

```
if (S.substring(k, k+1).equals(S.substring(j, j+1))) return true;
```

  and change line 6 to:

```
return false;
```

  D. Change line 3 to:

```
if (!(S.substring(k, k+1).equals(S.substring(j, j+1))) ||
    !(S.substring(k+1, k+2).equals(S.substring(j-1, j))))
    return false;
```

  E. Change line 3 to:

```
if (!(S.substring(k, k+1).equals(S.substring(j, j+1))) ||
    (j < k)) return false;
```

5. Consider the following methods:

```
public static void trySwap(int k, Integer K) {
    int tmp = K.intValue( );
    K = new Integer(k);
    k = tmp;
}

public static void test( ) {
    int n = 5;
    Integer N = new Integer(10);
    trySwap(n, N);
    System.out.println(n + " " + N);
}
```

What is output when method `test` executes?

A. 10 5

B. 5 5

C. 5 10

D. 10 10

E. Nothing is output; a `NullPointerException` is thrown when `trySwap` is called.

Answers to Multiple-Choice Questions

1. A
2. B
3. C
4. A
5. C

6.2   Interface and Class from the `java.util` Package

The `java.util.List<E>` Interface and the `java.util.ArrayList<E>` Class

The `List` interface is used for sequences of objects. The `ArrayList` class implements the `List` interface. An instance of the `ArrayList<E>` class represents a list (i.e., an ordered sequence) of items of type E. Like an array, elements can be accessed using their position in the list. Both the `ArrayList` class and the `List` interface are discussed in more detail in Chapter 4.

The AP CS Java subset includes the following `List<E>` and `ArrayList<E>` methods.

The `List<E>` Interface and the `ArrayList<E>` Class

`void add(E x)`	Adds x to the end of this list.
`void add(int n, E x)`	If index n is out of bounds (n < 0 or n > size()), throws an `IndexOutOfBoundsException`. Otherwise, moves the elements in positions n (counting from zero) to the end of this list over one place to the right to make room for new element x, then inserts x at position n in this list.
`E get(int n)`	If index n is out of bounds (n < 0 or n >= size()), throws an `IndexOutOfBoundsException`. Otherwise, returns the element at position n (counting from zero) in this list.
`E set(int n, E x)`	If index n is out of bounds (n < 0 or n >= size()), throws an `IndexOutOfBoundsException`. Otherwise, replaces the element at position n (counting from zero) in this list with x and returns the object that was previously at position n.
`int size()`	Returns the number of elements in this list.

Practice Multiple-Choice Questions

1. Consider writing code to return a random item from a non empty `ArrayList` called `myItems`. An outline of the code is given below.

   ```
   int k = (int)(Math.random() * <missing code 1>);
   return <missing code 2>;
   ```

   Which of the following are the best replacements for `<missing code 1>` and `<missing code 2>`?

	`<missing code 1>`	`<missing code 2>`
A.	`myItems.size() + 1`	`myItems(k).get(k)`
B.	`myItems.size() + 1`	`myItems.set(k)`
C.	`myItems.size()`	`myItems.get(k)`
D.	`myItems.size() - 1`	`myItems(k).remove(k)`
E.	`myItems.size()`	`myItems.remove(k)`

Questions 2 and 3 assume that variable a is an `ArrayList<String>` that has been initialized to contain a list of 10 strings.

2. Which of the following statements correctly adds the string `"the end"` to the end of the list?

Statement I	**Statement II**	**Statement III**
`a.add("the end");`	`a.add(10, "the end");`	`a.set(10, "the end");`

   A. I only
   B. II only
   C. I and II
   D. I and III
   E. II and III

3. Which of the following code segments correctly replaces the first string in the list with the string `"start"`?

   A. `a.set(0, "start");`
   B. `a.get(0, "start");`
   C. `a.add("start");`
   D. `a.add(0, "start");`
   E. `a.remove(0); a.add("start");`

Questions 4 and 5 concern the following situation: Two lists are used to keep track of information about the N students enrolled in a class. The information for each student is the student's (unique) ID number and the student's name (*more than one student may have the same name*). Variable names is a `List<String>` of size N that contains each of the students' names, and variable ids is a `List<String>` of size N that contains each of the students' ID numbers. For all values of k from 0 to $N-1$, the student whose name is in position k of the names list has the ID number that is in position k of the ids list.

4. Which of the following code segments correctly adds information for a new student?

Segment I	**Segment II**	**Segment III**
`names.add("Joe Sno");`	`names.add(0, "Joe Sno");`	`names.set(0, "Joe Sno");`
`ids.add("1234");`	`ids.add("1234");`	`ids.set(0, "1234");`

   A. I only
   B. II only
   C. III only
   D. I and II
   E. I and III

5.   Which of the following code segments returns `true` if and only if there is a student named Bobby Smith with ID number 2222 in the class?

I.
```
for (String id : ids) {
    if (id.equals("2222")) {
        return (names.get(id).equals("Bobby Smith"));
    }
}
return false;
```

II.
```
for (int k=0; k<ids.size(); k++) {
    if (ids.get(k).equals("2222") {
        return (names.get(k).equals("Bobby Smith"));
    }
}
return false;
```

III.
```
for (int k=0; k<names.size(); k++) {
    if (name.equals("Bobby Smith") {
        return (ids.get(k).equals("2222"));
    }
}
return false;
```

A. I only

B. II only

C. III only

D. I and II

E. I and III

Answers to Multiple-Choice Questions

1. E
2. C
3. A
4. A
5. B

7

Case Studies

Case studies are included in the AP Computer Science curriculum to give students the opportunity to study the development of a nontrivial piece of software; to understand how an expert would go about designing, implementing, and testing such software; and to practice the skills needed to understand and modify code written by someone else.

Each year, the AP CS exam includes both multiple-choice and free-response questions about a particular case study. Although a copy of the case study is available to students during the exam, it is absolutely vital that they already be familiar with the case study; there is not enough time during the exam to learn enough about the case study to be able to answer the questions.

If students have not worked with the current year's case study (the GridWorld Case Study), they should obtain a copy from the College Board Web site or by calling AP Order Fulfillment at: (800) 323-7155.

A summary of the GridWorld Case Study is given below.

7.1 Overview

The GridWorld Case Study is a large program designed to simulate *actors* (e.g., animals, flowers, and rocks) that inhabit and interact in a two-dimensional grid. It gives students practice with interfaces (including generic interfaces), classes (including generic classes), and inheritance.

The GridWorld Case Study includes different kinds of actors, whose interactions are governed by different rules. The GridWorld Case Study also includes two different kinds of grids (bounded and unbounded). A graphical user interface (GUI) is provided as part of the GridWorld Case Study, but the GUI will not be tested as part of the AP Examination.

The most important classes for students are the `Bug` and `Critter` classes (both subclasses of the `Actor` class). Students can expect to be tested on the implementations of these classes, as well as their subclasses `BoxBug` and `ChameleonCritter`. Students should also be familiar with the APIs for the `Grid` interface and for the following classes: `Actor`, `Flower`, `Rock`, and `Location`. Students should have a general understanding of how these classes and interfaces are used, and should be able to describe what each method of the class does, what are appropriate values for the parameters of each of the methods of the class, and how to use those methods in a larger problem.

7.2 The Actor Class

The Actor class is the heart of the GridWorld Case Study. Each actor keeps track of the following information:

1.   its grid
2.   its location in the grid
3.   its color
4.   the direction in which it is currently facing

The Actor class has one constructor and eleven public methods. The act method causes it to act; the other methods get and change its grid, location, color, and direction. The Actor constructor and methods are described below.

Method	Explanation
Constructor	The Actor class has one default (no-argument) constructor. It creates a blue actor facing north.
void act()	The act method causes the Actor to do whatever it is supposed to do during one step of the GridWorld simulation. The act method defined for the Actor class just reverses the direction of the actor. Subclasses are expected to override this method to define actors with more interesting behaviors.
Grid<Actor> getGrid()	The getGrid method returns the grid of this actor, or null if this actor is not in any grid.
Location getLocation()	The getLocation method returns the location of this actor in its grid, or null if this actor is not in any grid.
int getColor()	The getColor method returns the color of this actor.
int getDirection()	The getDirection method returns the direction of this actor: an angle between 0 and 359 degrees.
void putSelfInGrid(Grid<Actor> gr, Location loc)	The putSelfInGrid method puts this actor into location loc of grid gr. If there is another actor at that location, it is removed from the grid. The putSelfInGrid method has two preconditions: (1) this actor must not already be in a grid, and (2) loc must be a valid location in gr.
void removeSelfFromGrid()	The removeSelfFromGrid method removes this actor from its grid. There is one precondition: This actor is contained in a grid.

`void moveTo( Location newLocation )`	The `moveTo` method moves this actor to the given location in its grid. If there is another actor at that location, it is removed from the grid. The `moveTo` method has two preconditions: (1) this actor must be in a grid, and (2) `newLocation` must be a valid location in that grid.
`void setColor( Color newColor )`	The `setColor` method sets the color of this actor to `newColor`.
`void setDirection( int newDirection )`	The `setDirection` method changes the direction of this actor to the angle between 0 and 359 degrees that is equivalent to `newDirection`.
`String toString()`	The `toString` method returns a string with the location, direction, and color of this actor.

7.3 Subclasses of the `Actor` Class

As noted above, students are expected to be familiar with the implementations of two `Actor` subclasses: the `Bug` and `Critter` classes and their subclasses the `BoxBug` and `ChameleonCritter` classes. Students are also expected to be familiar with the APIs for the `Actor` subclasses `Flower` and `Rock`. These six classes are summarized below.

The `Bug` Class

The `Bug` class extends the `Actor` class: A bug is an actor whose `act` method causes it to move or to turn 45 degrees to the right. When it moves, it leaves behind a flower whose color matches its own.

The `Bug` class defines two new constructors, one with no parameters and the other with a single `Color` parameter. It also overrides the `Actor`'s `act` method, and defines three new methods used by the new `act` method: `canMove`, `move`, and `turn`.

The `Bug` Constructors and Methods

The `Bug`'s new no-argument constructor implicitly calls the `Actor` constructor (which creates a blue actor facing north), then sets the bug's color to red. The new one-argument constructor also implicitly calls the `Actor` constructor, then sets the bug's color to the value of its parameter.

The `Bug`'s new `act` method calls the `canMove` method to see whether the bug can move into the neighboring location toward which the bug is facing. A bug can move if all of the following conditions are satisfied:

- The bug is in a grid.
- The location into which the bug wants to move is valid (i.e., moving in that direction would not cause the bug to leave the grid).
- The location into which the bug wants to move is either empty or contains a flower.

If the bug can move, it calls the move method, which performs the following steps:

- Calls the moveTo method (inherited from the Actor class). The moveTo method moves the bug to the neighboring location. If that location was occupied (by a flower), it removes the flower from the grid.
- Creates a new flower object whose color matches the bug's color.
- Puts the new flower in the space just vacated by the bug.

If the bug cannot move, it calls the turn method, which turns the bug 45 degrees to the right.

The BoxBug Class

The BoxBug class extends the Bug class to define a bug that moves in a box shape. The size of the box is defined when the boxbug is created. The BoxBug class has two new fields: sideLength and steps. It uses those fields to keep track of the size of its box (the length of one side of the box), and how far along the current side of the box it has moved so far.

The BoxBug class defines a new one-argument constructor and overrides the Bug's act method. The new BoxBug constructor has one int parameter. This is the size of the bug's box (i.e., how many steps forward the boxbug is supposed to take before turning). The constructor implicitly calls the Bug no-argument constructor, then sets its steps field to zero and sets its sideLength field to the value of its parameter.

The BoxBug's act method first checks to see whether the boxbug has finished moving along the current side of its box. This is done by comparing the value of its steps and sideLength fields. It also calls the canMove method (inherited from the Bug class) to see whether the boxbug can continue moving straight ahead. If the boxbug has not yet finished one side of its box and it can move ahead, the act method causes the boxbug to move one step ahead by calling the move method (inherited from the Bug class). Otherwise, the act method causes the boxbug to turn 90 degrees to the right (by calling the turn method twice), and sets its steps field back to zero.

The Critter Class

The Critter class extends the Actor class: A critter is an actor whose act method causes it to consider a group of other actors, do something to them, then move to a new location. The Critter class overrides the Actor's act method and defines five new methods: getActors, processActors, getMoveLocations, selectMoveLocation, and makeMove.

The design of the Critter class has an important difference from the design of the Bug class: The intention is that subclasses of Bug will override the act method to define bugs that act differently. However, the intention is that subclasses of Critter will not override the act method; instead, they will override one or more of the five new methods defined in the Critter class (and listed above). This means that the way all critters act will follow the same general pattern defined in the Critter's act method.

The `Critter` Methods

The `Critter`'s new act method calls each of the five new `Critter` methods in turn:

1.   It calls the `getActors` method to get the group of actors that it wants to consider.

2.   It calls the `processActors` method to do something to the actors in the group.

3.   It calls the `getMoveLocations` method to get a list of locations in its grid.

4.   It calls the `selectMoveLocation` method (passing the list of locations returned by the `getMoveLocations` method) to choose a new location.

5.   It calls the `makeMove` method to move to the chosen new location.

Remember that subclasses of `Critter` are intended to override one or more of the five new `Critter` methods. Here are descriptions of how those methods work for the `Critter` class itself:

Method	Explanation
`getActors`	Returns all of the actors in this critter's neighboring locations.
`processActors`	Removes from the grid all of the actors returned by the `getActors` method that are neither rocks nor critters.
`getMoveLocations`	Returns all empty neighboring locations.
`selectMoveLocation`	Chooses randomly one of the locations returned by the `getMoveLocations` method.
`makeMove`	Moves this critter to the location selected by the `selectMoveLocation` method.

The `ChameleonCritter` Class

The `ChameleonCritter` class extends the `Critter` class. It overrides two of the `Critter` methods: `processActors` and `makeMove`. A chameleon critter doesn't remove any of its neighbors from the grid; instead, it randomly chooses one of their colors and changes its own color to match. The other difference between a critter and a chameleon critter is that when a chameleon critter moves, it also changes its direction so that it faces the direction in which it moves.

The `Flower` Class

The `Flower` class is a subclass of the `Actor` class. Only the API is tested on the AP Examination.

The `Flower` class defines one default (no-argument) constructor and one constructor with a `Color` parameter. It also overrides the `Actor`'s act method. The `Flower` default constructor creates a pink flower. The other constructor creates a flower with the given color.

The `Flower`'s act method causes the color of the flower to darken.

The Rock **Class**

The Rock class is a subclass of the Actor class. Only the API is tested on the AP Examination.

The Rock class defines one default (no-argument) constructor and one constructor with a Color parameter. It also overrides the Actor's act method. The Rock default constructor creates a black rock. The other constructor creates a rock with the given color.

The Rock's act method does nothing.

7.4   Locations and Grids

In the GridWorld Case Study, actors are stored in locations in grids. Each actor keeps track of its grid and its location in that grid. Locations are implemented using the Location class. Grids are implemented using the Grid interface and the AbstractGrid, BoundedGrid, and UnboundedGrid classes. Students may be tested on the API for the Grid interface, including the concepts of bounded and unbounded grids.

The Grid **Interface**

There are two kinds of grids: bounded and unbounded. Both have rows and columns. A bounded grid has a fixed number of rows and columns, and they are both numbered starting from zero (like a two-dimensional array). A number in the range zero to one less than the number of rows in the grid is a *valid* row number, and a number in the range zero to one less than the number of columns in the grid is a *valid* column number.

An unbounded grid should be thought of as having an infinite number of rows and columns. Any integer value (negative, zero, or positive) is a valid row or column number in an unbounded grid.

The Grid interface is a generic interface with one type parameter that specifies the type of the objects that will be stored in the grid: Grid<E>. Each grid keeps track of how many rows and columns it has, and what objects are currently stored in the grid. It provides the following 11 methods:

Method	Explanation
int getNumRows()	Returns the number of rows in this grid if it is a bounded grid. Otherwise, returns −1.
int getNumCols()	Returns the number of columns in this grid if it is a bounded grid. Otherwise, returns −1.
boolean isValid(Location loc)	Returns true if loc is a valid location in this grid. *Precondition*: loc is not null.
E put(Location loc, E obj)	Puts obj at location loc in this grid, and returns the object previously in that location (or null if that location was empty). *Precondition*: loc is a valid location in this grid and obj is not null.

`E remove(Location loc)`	If location `loc` is occupied, removes and returns the object in that location. Otherwise, returns `null`. *Precondition*: `loc` is a valid location in this grid.
`E get(Location loc)`	Returns the object at location `loc` or `null` if that location is not occupied. *Precondition*: `loc` is a valid location in this grid.
`ArrayList<Location>` `  getOccupiedLocations()`	Returns a list of all occupied locations in this grid.

`ArrayList<Location>`
`  getValidAdjacentLocations(`
`Location loc)`
	Returns a list of the valid locations in this grid that are adjacent to location `loc`. *Precondition*: `loc` is a valid location in this grid.

`ArrayList<Location>`
`  getEmptyAdjacentLocations`
`(Location loc)`
	Returns a list of the valid locations in this grid that are adjacent to location `loc` and are empty. *Precondition*: `loc` is a valid location in this grid.

`ArrayList<Location> getOccupied` `AdjacentLocations(Location loc)`	Returns a list of the valid locations in this grid that are adjacent to location `loc` and are occupied. *Precondition*: `loc` is a valid location in this grid.
`ArrayList<E> getNeighbors(` `Location loc)`	Returns a list of the objects that are in occupied locations adjacent to location `loc`. *Precondition*: `loc` is a valid location in this grid.

The `Location` Class

The GridWorld Case Study defines the `Location` class to represent the locations in a grid. Each location keeps track of its row and column numbers. The `Location` class implements the `Comparable` interface. It provides the following constructor and methods.

Method	Explanation
`Location(int r, int c)`	This constructor creates a location with row number `r` and column number `c`.
`int getRow()`	Returns this location's row number.
`int getCol()`	Returns this location's column number.

`getAdjacentLocation`
`  (int direction)`
	Returns the adjacent location in the direction that is closest to its `direction` parameter. Directions are integer values that represent angles from north. The value 0 means north, 45 means northeast, 90 means east, and so on. The `Location` class defines constants for the eight compass directions:
	`Location.NORTH,  Location.NORTHEAST,`
	`Location.EAST,   Location.SOUTHEAST,`
	`Location.SOUTH,  Location.SOUTHWEST,`
	`Location.WEST,   Location.NORTHWEST.`

`int getDirectionToward(` `Location target)`	Returns the closest direction from this location towards `target`.

`boolean equals(Object other)`	Returns `true` if `other` is a `Location` with the same row and column numbers as this location. Otherwise, returns `false`.
`int compareTo(Object other)`	Returns a negative integer if this location is less than `other` (has a lower row number, or has the same row number and a lower column number); returns zero if this location has the same row and column numbers as `other`; otherwise, returns a positive number. This method has a precondition that `other` is a `Location`.
`String toString()`	Returns a `String` in the format "(r, c)", where r is this location's row number and c is its column number.

7.5   Test-Taking Hints

Following are some simple suggestions that can be helpful when answering multiple-choice or free-response questions based on the case study.

- Use the Case-Study Quick Reference. Do not assume that you remember the exact names of methods, the order of their parameters, or the classes to which they belong. Double-checking in the quick reference can help eliminate small errors that could cost you points.

- If you are asked to reimplement a method that already exists, look up that method in the quick reference. You will find the code from the original implementation and it could help you in implementing a change.

- Read the directions carefully. The question may tell you to assume that some methods other than the ones you are being asked to write have been modified. Your code must take those other modifications into account.

- Double-check your code to make sure you have satisfied all of the requirements of the question. Often there is a final step that updates either the current object or another object; be sure not to omit that final step.

Practice Multiple-Choice Questions

1. Assume that variable `grid` is a properly initialized `Grid`. Which of the following expressions evaluates to the number of occupied locations in `grid`?

   A. `grid.numRows() * grid.numCols()`

   B. `grid.getOccupiedLocations()`

   C. `grid.getOccupiedLocations().size()`

   D. `grid.getOccupiedAdjacentLocations().size()`

   E. `grid.toString().size()`

2. Assume that variable oneBug is a bug facing north in its grid. Under which of the following conditions would the method call oneBug.canMove() return true?

I. The location to the north of the bug is empty.
II. The location to the north of the bug contains a flower.
III. The location to the north of the bug contains a rock.

A. I only

B. II only

C. III only

D. I and II

E. II and III

3. Which of the following methods is defined in the Bug class because it is required to correctly extend the Actor class?

A. act

B. turn

C. move

D. canMove

E. No methods are required to be implemented in the Bug class to correctly extend the Actor class.

4. Consider implementing a new subclass of Critter called FlowerCritter. The way a FlowerCritter acts is to first remove from the grid all other actors that are not flowers. Then it moves to an empty location adjacent to a flower. If there are no flowers in the grid, or no empty location adjacent to a flower, the FlowerCritter removes itself from its grid.

Which of the following Critter methods would *not* need to be over ridden in the FlowerCritter class?

A. getActors

B. processActors

C. getMoveLocations

D. selectMoveLocation

E. makeMove

5. Assume that the following code has been executed,

```
BoxBug abug = new BoxBug(3);
```

and that the new BoxBug is placed in the grid as shown below (where B means the BoxBug, F means a Flower, and R means a Rock).

B		F	
			R

Which of the following shows the path that abug would follow?

A.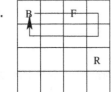

D.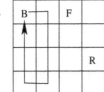

B.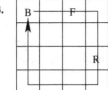

E.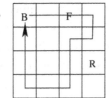

C.

B⌐	F		
		R	

Answers to Multiple-Choice Questions

1. C
2. D
3. E
4. E
5. A

PRACTICE EXAMINATIONS

Hints for Students

This section contains a few practical hints that may help you improve your performance on the AP Computer Science exam.

Multiple-Choice Questions

Hint 1

When the multiple-choice questions are graded, one-quarter of a point is subtracted for each wrong answer to compensate for guessing. Therefore, if you have no idea what the answer to a multiple-choice question is, you are probably better off skipping the question than just guessing. However, if you are able to eliminate one or more responses as definitely not the right answer, it is a good idea to make a guess among the remaining responses.

Hint 2

Many multiple-choice questions involve some code. It is usually better to look first at the question itself, rather than studying the code. Knowing what is being addressed by the question (e.g., what does the code do, what value is produced by executing the code on a particular input, or which line of code contains an error) will help you to focus on the important aspects of the code without wasting time trying to understand every detail.

Hint 3

Sometimes multiple-choice questions are grouped: two or three questions are asked about a common "preamble," which might, for example, be a piece of code or an explanation of a choice of data structures. Do not give up on the whole group of questions just because you are not able to answer the first question in the group! The second question may be easier; it may even give you a new insight that will help you answer the first question. (And remember, as suggested in hint 2 above, it is usually best to look at the actual questions before spending a lot of time reading the preamble.)

Free-Response Questions

Hint 1

The criteria for grading the free-response questions are determined by the chief faculty consultant, so some changes may occur from year to year. The current philosophy is that the score for a free-response question depends on whether the code works correctly. Syntactic details, programming style, and efficiency are very minor issues. Leaving out a few semicolons will not affect the score; neither will using one-character variable names. Comments are not necessary; however, including brief comments may help you to organize your thoughts and may make it easier for you to check your work. Unless the question specifically addresses the issue of efficiency, it is better to write simple, clear code than to write complicated, super-efficient code.

Note that code written in a language other than Java will probably receive no credit.

Hint 2

Free-response questions are often divided into several parts, each of which involves writing a method. The instructions for one part of the question may include something like this:

> In writing method XXX, you may include calls to method YYY, specified above in part (a).

It will usually (though not always) be easier for you to write method XXX if you do indeed include calls to method YYY. If it isn't immediately obvious to you how to use method YYY, spend a few minutes thinking about a different approach to writing method XXX that involves calls to YYY. This may save you time in the long run, because the version of XXX that uses YYY may be easier to write than the version you originally thought of.

Hint 3

If you are asked to write a method with a non-void return type, don't forget to return a value of the correct type.

Practice Examination A-1

Section I

Time: 1 hour and 15 minutes
Number of questions: 40
Percent of total grade: 50

1. The expression

   ```
   !(a || b)
   ```

   is equivalent to which of the following expressions?

   A. (a || b)
   B. (!a) || (!b)
   C. (!a) && (!b)
   D. !(a && b)
   E. (a || b) && (a && b)

2. Which of the following statements about classes and interfaces is true?

   A. A class can extend at most one other class, but can implement more than one interface.

   B. A class can extend more than one other class and can implement more than one interface.

   C. A class can extend more than one other class, but can implement at most one interface.

   D. A class *must* extend another class and *must* implement at least one interface.

   E. A class need not extend another class but *must* implement at least one interface.

Questions 3–5 concern the following (incomplete) definition of the PosSeq class, which will be used to represent a sequence of positive integer values. Line numbers for the search method are included for reference for question 5.

```
public class PosSeq {
   private int[] seq;

   // constructor
   public PosSeq( int seqLength ) {
      int val;
      seq = new int[seqLength];
      for (int k=0; k<seqLength; k++) {
         System.out.print("Enter a positive number: ");
         : missing code
         seq[k] = val;
      }
   }

   public int getMax() {
   // precondition: seq.length > 0
      int final = value;
      for (int k=1; k<seq.length; k++) {
         if (seq[k] > final) statement
      }
      return final;
   }
```

```
1    public boolean search(int key) {
2       int k=0;
3       while ((k < seq.length) && (seq[k] != key)) k++;
4       if (seq[k] == key) return true;
5       return false;
6    }
   }
```

3. The constructor for the `PosSeq` class is supposed to be an *interactive* method that initializes the `seq` array using positive numbers typed in by the person running the program. Assume that the method `readInt` reads and returns one integer value typed in by the user. Which of the following is the best replacement for the placeholder *missing code* in the `PosSeq` constructor?

A. `val = readInt();`

B. `val = readInt();`
   `if (val <= 0) val = 1;`

C. `val = readInt();`
   `if (val <= 0) System.out.println("Bad input.");`

D. `val = readInt();`
   `while (val <= 0) {`
   `    val = readInt();`
   `}`

E. `val = readInt();`
   `while (val <= 0) {`
   `    System.out.println("Bad input");`
   `    System.out.print("Enter a positive number: ");`
   `    val = readInt();`
   `}`

4. Which of the following replacements for *value* and *statement* could be used to complete the `getMax` method so that it returns the largest value in the `seq` array?

	value	*statement*
A.	0	`final = k;`
B.	0	`final = seq[k];`
C.	`seq[0]`	`final = k;`
D.	`seq[0]`	`final = seq[k];`
E.	`k`	`final = k;`

5. The `search` method was intended to return `true` if and only if the given key value is in the `seq` array. However, the method is not written correctly. Which of the following statements about this method is true?

A. There will be an error when the method is compiled because the `&&` operator used on line 3 is applied to a nonboolean expression.

B. The test "(`seq[k] != key`)" on line 3 will cause an `IndexOutOfBounds Exception` whenever `seq` contains the value `key`.

C. The test "(`seq[k] != key`)" on line 3 will cause an `IndexOutOfBounds Exception` whenever `seq` does *not* contain the value `key`.

D. The test "`seq[k] == key`" on line 4 will cause an `IndexOutOfBoundsException` whenever `seq` contains the value `key`.

E. The test "`seq[k] == key`" on line 4 will cause an `IndexOutOfBoundsException` whenever `seq` does *not* contain the value `key`.

6. Consider writing a method whose sole purpose is to write an error message using System.out.print. Which of the following best characterizes the choice between making the method's return type void and making it int?

   A. The return type should be void because the method performs an operation and does not compute a value.

   B. The return type should be int because that is the default return type for Java methods.

   C. The return type should be void because void methods are more efficient than int methods.

   D. The return type should be int because int methods are more efficient than void methods.

   E. The return type should be void because the method does not need to be recursive.

7. Consider the following instance variable and method:

```java
private ArrayList<Object> myList;

public boolean compare(ArrayList<Object> A) {
    for (Object ob : myList) {
        int k = A.size()-1;
        while (k >= 0 && !ob.equals(A.get(k))) k--;
        if (k < 0) return false;
    }
    return true;
}
```

   Which of the following best describes when method compare returns true?

   A. When A includes at least one copy of every object in myList.

   B. When A contains the same objects as myList in the same order.

   C. When A contains the same objects as myList in reverse order.

   D. When A contains the same objects as myList either in the same order or in reverse order.

   E. Never.

Questions 8 and 9 refer to the following definition of the Person class.

```
public class Person {
   private String firstName;
   private String lastName;
   private int age;

   // constructor
   public Person( String fn, String ln, int a ) {
     firstName = fn;
     lastName = ln;
     age = a;
   }
   public String getFirstName() { return firstName; }
   public String getLastName() { return lastName; }
   public int getAge() { return age; }
}
```

8. Assume that a variable P has been declared as follows:

    ```
    Person[] P;
    ```

    and that P has been initialized with data for 20 people. Which of the following correctly tests whether the third person's age is greater than 10?

    A. `P.getAge[2] > 10`

    B. `P.Person[2] > 10`

    C. `P[2].Person.getAge() > 10`

    D. `P[2].getAge() > 10`

    E. `P.Person.getAge[2] > 10`

9. Assume that variables p1 and p2 have been declared as follows:

    ```
    Person p1, p2;
    ```

    Which of the following is the best way to test whether the people represented by p1 and p2 have the same first name?

    A. `p1 == p2`

    B. `p1.getFirstName().equals(p2.getFirstName())`

    C. `p1.getFirstName() == p2.getFirstName()`

    D. `p1.equals(p2)`

    E. `p2.equals(p1)`

Questions 10 and 11 concern the design of a data structure to store information about which seats on an airplane are reserved. The airplane has N rows (where N is some large number); each row has four seats. Two data structures are being considered:

Data Structure 1: An array of Rows, where a Row is a class with four boolean fields, one for each seat in the row. The length of the array is N. The fields of the kth element in the array are true if and only if the corresponding seats in row k are reserved.

Data Structure 2: An array of Reservations, where a Reservation is a class with two integer fields: a row number and a seat number. The length of the array is initially 0. Each time a seat is reserved, a new array is allocated, containing one more element than the previous array; the old array is copied over into the new array, and then the last element of the array is filled in with the newly reserved seat's row and number.

10. Assume that an int and a boolean require the same amount of space. Under which of the following conditions does data structure 1 require less space than data structure 2?

   A. No seats are reserved.

   B. All seats are reserved.

   C. Only the seats in the first row are reserved.

   D. Only the seats in the last row are reserved.

   E. Data structure 1 never requires less space than data structure 2.

11. Which of the following operations can be implemented more efficiently using data structure 1 than using data structure 2?

   Operation I: Determine how many seats are reserved.

   Operation II: Determine whether all seats in a particular row (given the row number) are reserved.

   Operation III: Reserve a seat on a half-full airplane, given the row and seat numbers.

   A. I only

   B. II only

   C. III only

   D. I and II

   E. II and III

12. Which of the following statements about a method's preconditions is true?

    A. They must be provided by the writer of the method or the method will not compile.

    B. They are translated by the compiler into runtime checks.

    C. They provide information to users of the method, specifying what is expected to be true whenever the method is called.

    D. They provide information to the writer of the method, specifying how it is to be implemented.

    E. They provide information about the class that contains the method.

13. Assume that variable A has type `ArrayList<Integer>`. Consider the following code segment:

```
boolean flag = false;
for (Integer oneInt : A) {
    flag = flag && (oneInt.intValue() > 0);
}
```

Which of the following best describes what this code segment does?

    A. Always sets `flag` to `true`.

    B. Always sets `flag` to `false`.

    C. Sets `flag` to `true` if every value in A is positive.

    D. Sets `flag` to `true` if any value in A is positive.

    E. Sets `flag` to `true` if the last value in A is positive.

14. Consider the following code segment:

```
x = !y;
y = x || y;
```

Assume that x and y are boolean variables that have been initialized before this code executes. What is true about the values of x and y after the code executes?

    A. Variable x is `true`.

    B. Variable y is `true`.

    C. Variable x has the same value as it did before the code executed.

    D. Variable y has the same value as it did before the code executed.

    E. Variable y has the same value as variable x had before the code executed.

Questions 15 and 16 refer to the following incomplete definitions of the `Person` and `Child` classes (note that `Child` is a subclass of `Person`).

```
public class Person {
   private String name;
   private int age;

   // constructor
   public Person(String n, int a) {
      name = n;
      age = a;
   }

   // other methods not shown
}


public class Child extends Person {
   private String school;

   // constructor
   public Child(String n, int a, String s) {
      : missing code
   }

   public String getSchool() {
      return school;
   }
}
```

15. Which of the following replacements for *missing code* in the `Child` class constructor would compile without error?

    A. `super(n, a);`
        `school = s;`
    B. `school = s;`
        `super(n, a);`
    C. `name = n;`
        `age = a;`
        `school = s;`
    D. `super(n);`
        `age = a;`
        `school = s;`
    E. `super(n, a, s);`

16. Assume that the `Child` constructor has been defined correctly. Consider the following code segment.

```
Person p = new Child("Chris", 10, "Lincoln School");
System.out.println(p.getSchool());
```

Which of the following statements about this code segment is true?

A. It will not compile because the type of p is `Person`, and class `Person` has no `getSchool` method.

B. It will not compile because the type of p is `Person`, and the type of the value assigned to p is `Child`.

C. It will compile, but there will be a runtime error when the first line is executed because the type of p is `Person`, and the type of the value assigned to p is `Child`.

D. It will compile, but there will be a runtime error when the second line is executed because the type of p is `Person`, and class `Person` has no `getSchool` method.

E. It will compile and run without error, and will print `Lincoln School`.

17. Consider the following recursive method:

```
public static void printStars(int k) {
    if (k>0) {
        printStars(k-1);
        for (int j=1; j<=k; j++) System.out.print("*");
        System.out.println();
    }
}
```

What is output as a result of the call `printStars(4)`?

A. ****
***
**
*

B. *
**
***
****

C. ***
**
*

D. *
**
***

E. *
*
*
*

18. Consider the following instance variable and method:

```
private ArrayList<Integer> L;

public int listSum() {
// precondition: L contains one or more positive integers
    int sum = 0;
    for (Integer oneInteger : L) {
        int oneInt = oneInteger.intValue();
        if ((Integer.MAX_VALUE - oneInt) < sum) {
            return 0;
        }
        sum += oneInt;
    }
    return sum;
}
```

Which of the following best explains what method listSum does?

A. Always returns 0.

B. Always returns the sum of the values in L.

C. Always returns the number of values in L.

D. Returns 0 if the sum of the values in L is too big; otherwise, returns the sum of the values in L.

E. Returns 0 if there are too many values in L; otherwise, returns the number of values in L.

19. Consider writing a program to be used by a car dealership to keep track of information about the cars they sell. For each car, they would like to keep track of the model number, the price, and the miles per gallon the car gets in the city and on the highway. Which of the following is the best way to represent the information?

A. Define one class, Car, with four fields: modelNumber, price, cityMilesPerGallon, and highwayMilesPerGallon.

B. Define one superclass, Car, with four subclasses: ModelNumber, Price, CityMilesPerGallon, and HighwayMilesPerGallon.

C. Define five unrelated classes: Car, ModelNumber, Price, CityMilesPerGallon, and HighwayMilesPerGallon.

D. Define five classes: Car, ModelNumber, Price, CityMilesPerGallon, and HighwayMilesPerGallon. Make HighwayMilesPerGallon a subclass of CityMilesPerGallon, make CityMilesPerGallon a subclass of Price, make Price a subclass of ModelNumber, and make ModelNumber a subclass of Car.

E. Define five classes: Car, ModelNumber, Price, CityMilesPerGallon, and Highway-MilesPerGallon. Make Car a subclass of ModelNumber, make Model Number a subclass of Price, make Price a subclass of CityMilesPerGallon, and make CityMilesPerGallon a subclass of HighwayMilesPerGallon.

20. Consider using binary search to look for a given value in an array of integers. Which of the following must be true in order for the search to work?

   I.   The values in the array are stored in sorted order.

   II. The array does not contain any duplicate values.

   III. The array does not contain any negative values.

   A. I only

   B. II only

   C. III only

   D. I and II

   E. II and III

Questions 21–24 involve reasoning about the GridWorld Case Study.

21. Which of the following classes implements the `Comparable` interface?

   A. `Actor`
   B. `Bug`
   C. `Critter`
   D. `Grid`
   E. `Location`

22. Consider defining a new class called `SillyBug` that extends the Bug class. Assume that a SillyBug has two fields:

   ```
   private BoxBug myBoxBug;
   private int numLegs;
   ```

   Including which of the following statements in a `SillyBug` method would cause a compile-time error?

   A. `numLegs = myBoxBug.steps;`
   B. `numLegs = myBoxBug.getDirection();`
   C. `myBoxBug.setColor(getColor());`
   D. `myBoxBug.setDirection(numLegs);`
   E. `myBoxBug.removeSelfFromGrid();`

23. Consider defining a new class called `NewBug` that extends the Bug class. Assume that a constructor for the NewBug class is written that has three parameters: `Grid<Actor> gr`, `Location loc`, `Color col`. Which of the following could be the body of the NewBug constructor?

   A. `super(gr, loc, col);`
   B. `super(col);`
      `putSelfInGrid(gr, loc);`
   C. `super(col);`
      `putSelfInGrid(gr);`
   D. `super(gr, loc);`
      `setColor(col);`
   E. `super(gr);`
      `moveTo(loc);`
      `setColor(col);`

24. Consider changing the Grid interface by replacing the isValid method with two new methods:

isValidRow(int r) Returns true if r is a valid row number in this grid; otherwise, returns false.

isValidCol(int c) Returns true if c is a valid column number in this grid; otherwise, returns false.

Which of the following statements about the changes that would be needed to the Bug class is true?

A. No changes would be needed.

B. None of the methods defined in the Bug class would need to be changed, but the putSelfInGrid method would need to be overridden.

C. Only the act method would need to be changed.

D. Only the move and canMove methods would need to be changed.

E. All of the Bug methods would need to be changed.

25. Consider the following code segment. Assume that method readInt reads and returns one integer value.

```
int x;
int sumNeg=0;
int sumPos=0;
x = readInt();
while (x != 0) {
   if (x < 0)
      sumNeg += x;
   if (x > 0)
      sumPos += x;
   x = readInt();
}
if (sumNeg < -8)
   System.out.println("negative sum: " + sumNeg);
if (sumPos > 8)
   System.out.println("positive sum: " + sumPos);
```

Which of the following inputs causes every line of code to be executed at least once?

A. 0

B. 2   4   6   8   0

C. 2   −2   4   −4   0

D. 4   −4   6   −6   0

E. −2   −4   −6   −8   0

26. Assume that a program has been run on an input that caused every line of code to be executed at least once. Also assume that there were no runtime errors and that the program produced the correct output. Which of the following is a valid assumption?

A. If the program is changed only by rearranging lines of code, and then run on the same input, there will be no runtime errors, and the program will produce the correct output.

B. If the program is changed only by removing one line of code, and then run on the same input, there will be no runtime errors, and the program will produce the correct output.

C. If the program is run on a different input, there will be no runtime errors, and the program will produce the correct output.

D. If the program is run on a different input, there will be no runtime errors, but the program might produce incorrect output.

E. None of the above assumptions is valid.

Questions 27 and 28 refer to the following `arraySum` method.

```
public int arraySum( int A[][] ) {
    int sum = 0;
    for (int row=0; row<A.length; row++) {
        for (int col=0; col<A.length; col++) {
            sum += A[row][col];
        }
    }
    return sum;
}
```

The `arraySum` method was intended to return the sum of the values in its array parameter A. However, when it was tested, it was discovered that it sometimes returns the wrong value and sometimes causes an `IndexOutOfBoundsException`

27. For which of the following arrays would `arraySum` return the wrong value?

| I. | II. | III. |

| 5 | 2 | 4 | 6 |
| 4 | 4 | 1 | 2 |

| 1 | 2 |
| 0 | 3 |

2	3
4	5
6	7
8	9

A. I only

B. II only

C. III only

D. I and II

E. I and III

28. For which of the following arrays would `arraySum` cause an `IndexOutOfBoundsException`?

I.

5	2	4	6
4	4	1	2

II.

1	2
0	3

III.

2	3
4	5
6	7
8	9

A. I only

B. II only

C. III only

D. I and II

E. I and III

29. Consider the following code segment:

```
ArrayList<String> L = new ArrayList<String>();
for (int k=1; k<6; k++) {
    if (k%2 == 0) L.add("?");
    else L.add("!");
}
```

Which of the following correctly illustrates the list represented by `ArrayList L` after this code segment executes?

A. `[?, ?, ?, ?, ?]`

B. `[!, !, !, !, !]`

C. `[!, ?, !, ?, !]`

D. `[?, !, ?, !, ?]`

E. `[?, ?, !, ?, ?]`

30. Consider the following instance variable and method, with line numbers included in the method for reference.

```
   private String word;

1  public String oddChars(String word) {
2      String result = "";
3      for (int k=0; k<word.length(); k+=2) {
4          result += word.substring(k, k);
5      }
6      return result;
7  }
```

Method oddChars was intended to return a string that contains every other character in word, starting with the first character. For example, if word is "abcd", oddChars should return "ac"; and if word is "abcde", it should return "ace". However, when the method is tested, it is discovered that it always returns an empty string.

Which of the following would fix method oddChars?

A. Change the for-loop initialization on line 3 from k=0 to k=1

B. Change the for-loop stopping condition on line 3 from k<word.length() to k<=word.length()

C. Change the for-loop increment on line 3 from k+=2 to k++

D. Change line 4 to result += word.substring(k, k+1);

E. Change line 4 to result += word.substring(k);

Questions 31–33 refer to the following Location class.

```java
public class Location {
    private String name;
    private double latitude;
    private double longitude;

    // constructor
    public Location(String n, double lat, double lon) {
        name = n;
        latitude = lat;
        longitude = lon;
    }

    public String getName() {
        return name;
    }

    public void setName(String n) {
        name = n;
    }

    public boolean equals(Object other) {
        return (latitude == ((Location)other).latitude &&
                longitude == ((Location)other).longitude);
    }
}
```

31. Assume that variables L1, L2, and L3 have been declared and initialized as follows:

```java
Location L1 = new Location("Baltimore", 39.18, 76.38);
Location L2 = new Location("Baltimore", 39.18, 76.38);
Location L3 = new Location("Albany",    39.18, 76.38);
```

Which of the following expressions evaluate to true?

I.   L1.equals(L2)
II. L2.equals(L3)
III. L1 == L2

A. I only

B. II only

C. III only

D. I and II

E. I and III

32. Consider the following code segment.

```
Location L1 = new Location("Baltimore", 39.18, 76.38);
Location L2 = L1;
Location L3 = L1;
L1.setName("NewYork");
L2.setName("Chicago");
System.out.print(L1.getName() + " " + L2.getName() +
                 " " + L3.getName());
```

What is printed when the code executes?

A. NewYork NewYork NewYork

B. Chicago Chicago Chicago

C. NewYork Chicago Baltimore

D. Chicago Chicago Baltimore

E. NewYork Chicago Baltimore

33. Consider the following instance variable and incomplete method:

```
private Location[] locList;

public boolean locWithName(String name) {
// precondition: neither name nor locList is null
// postcondition: returns true iff there is a location in locList
//                with the given name
   for (int k=0; k<locList.length; k++) {
      if ( condition ) return true;
   }
   return false;
}
```

Which of the following could be used to replace *condition* so that method `locWithName` works as specified by its pre- and postconditions?

A. name.equals(locList[k].getName())

B. name.equals(locList.getName()[k])

C. name == locList.getName[k]

D. name == locList[k].getName()

E. name == locList[k]

34. Consider the following interface definition:

```
public interface Employee {
   public double getSalary();
   public void setSalary( double newSalary );
}
```

Which of the following is a correct implementation of the Employee interface?

A. ```
public class Person implements Employee {
   public double getSalary;
   public void setSalary;
}
```

B. ```
public class Person implements Employee {
   public double getSalary() { return salary; }
   public void setSalary( double newSalary ) {
      salary = newSalary;
   }
}
```

C. ```
public class Person implements Employee {
   private double salary;

   public double getSalary() { return salary; }
}
```

D. ```
public class Person implements Employee {
   private double salary;

   public double getSalary() { return salary; }
   public void setSalary( double newSalary ) {
      salary = newSalary;
   }
}
```

E. ```
public class Person implements Employee {
   private double salary;

   private double getSalary() { return salary; }
   private void setSalary(double newSalary) {
      salary = newSalary;
   }
}
```
```

35. Assume that a class includes the following three methods:

```
public static int min(int x, int y) {
    if (x < y) return x;
    else return y;
}

public static int min(String s, String t) {
    if (s.length() < t.length()) return s.length();
    else return t.length();
}

public static void testMin() {
    System.out.println(min(3, "hello"));
}
```

Which of the following best describes what happens when this code is compiled and executed?

A. The code will not compile because the types of the arguments used in the call to `min` do not match the types of the parameters in either version of `min`.

B. The code will not compile because it includes two methods with the same name and the same return type.

C. The code will not compile because it includes two methods with the same name and the same number of parameters.

D. The code will compile and execute without error; the output will be 3.

E. The code will compile and execute without error; the output will be 5.

36. Which of the following code segments sets variable sum to be the sum of the even numbers between 1 and 99?

   A.
```
int k;
int sum = 0;
for (k=1; k<=99; k++) {
    if (k%2 == 0) sum++;
}
```

   B.
```
int k;
int sum = 0;
for (k=1; k<=99; k++) {
    if (k%2 == 0) sum += k;
}
```

   C.
```
int k = 1;
int sum = 0;
while (k <= 99) {
    sum += k;
    k += 2;
}
```

   D.
```
int k = 2;
int sum = 0;
while (k <= 99) {
    sum++;
    k += 2;
}
```

   E.
```
int k = 2;
int sum = 0;
while (k <= 99) {
    k += 2;
    sum += k;
}
```

37. Consider the following code segment:

```
String[] myStrings = new String[3];
myStrings[0] = "abc";
myStrings[1] = myStrings[0];
myStrings[0] = "xxx";
myStrings[2] = myStrings[1] + "XYZ";
for (int k=0; k<3; k++) System.out.print(myStrings[k] + " ");
```

What is printed when this code executes?

   A. xxx xxx xxxXYZ

   B. xxx abc abcXYZ

   C. abcxxx abc abcxxxXYZ

   D. xxx xxx xxxZYZ

   E. abcxxx abcxxx abcxxxXYZ

38. Consider the following (incomplete) method:

```
public void changeOb( Object value ) {
    ⋮
}
```

Assume that variable k is an `int`, that variable s is a `String`, and that variable ob is an `Object`. Which of the following calls to method changeOb will compile without error?

Call I	**Call II**	**Call III**
changeOb(k);	changeOb(s);	changeOb(ob);

A. I only

B. II only

C. III only

D. I and II

E. II and III

Questions 39 and 40 concern the following recursive method:

```
public int mystery(int k) {
    if (k == 1) return 0;
    else return(1 + mystery(k/2));
}
```

39. What value is returned by the call mystery(16)?

A. 0

B. 2

C. 4

D. 5

E. No value is returned because the call causes an infinite recursion.

40. Which of the following best characterizes the values of k for which the call mystery(k) leads to an infinite recursion?

A. No values

B. All positive values

C. All nonpositive values

D. All odd values

E. All even values

Section II

Time: 1 hour and 45 minutes
Number of questions: 4
Percent of total grade: 50

Question 1

This question involves reasoning about the code from the GridWorld Case Study.

Consider implementing a new subclass of Actor as part of the GridWorld Case Study. This new actor will be a Gardener and will act as follows:

- The Gardener will go home (remove herself from her grid) if she has been gardening for more than 30 time steps (as recorded by her private steps field) or if she has been gardening for more than 10 time steps and the number of flowers she has picked is less than .1 times the number of time steps she has been gardening.

- If the Gardener does not go home, she will move as follows and then increment the number of time steps she has been gardening.

    - She will check her neighboring locations to determine if she has any flower neighbors.
    - If there are flower neighbors, she will:

        - Choose one of the flowers at random.
        - Pick that flower (by having it remove itself from the grid).
        - Increment the number of flowers she has picked.
        - Move to a random, empty, neighboring location.

    - If there are no flower neighbors, she will move randomly into a neighboring location, removing whatever object (if any) is in that location.

An incomplete declaration of the Gardener class is shown on the next page.

```
public class Gardener extends Actor {

  private int steps;
  private int flowersPicked;

  /*
   * Finds all neighboring locations that contain a flower
   * Precondition: This Gardener is in a Grid.
   * Postcondition: Returns an ArrayList containing the locations of
   *                all neighboring flowers.  If there are no flower
   *                neighbors, an empty ArrayList is returned.
   */
  private ArrayList<Location> getFlowerNeighbors() { /* part (a) */ }

  /*
   * If there is at least one neighboring flower, pick a random
   * neighboring flower, increment the number of flowers picked, and
   * move into a random neighboring empty location.
   * Otherwise, move to a random neighboring location, removing
   * whatever object (if any) is in that location.
   */
  public void move() { /* part (b) */ }

  /*
   * If this gardener has been gardening for more than 30 time steps
   * or if she has been gardening for more than 10 time steps and the
   * number of flowers she has picked is less .1 times the number of
   * time steps she has been gardening, then she will remove herself
   * from her grid.
   * Otherwise, she will move (which includes picking a neighboring
   * flower if there is one), then she will increment the number of
   * time steps she has been gardening.
   */
  public void act() { /* part (c) */ }

  // other methods not shown
}
```

Part (a)

Write the Gardener method getFlowerNeighbors, which returns an ArrayList containing the locations of the flowers adjacent to the Gardener, or an empty ArrayList if there are no neighboring flowers.

Complete method getFlowerNeighbors below.

```
/*
 * Finds all neighboring locations that contain a flower
 * Precondition: This Gardener is in a Grid.
 * Postcondition: Returns an ArrayList containing the locations of
 *                all neighboring flowers.  If there are no flower
 *                neighbors, an empty ArrayList is returned.
 */
private ArrayList<Location> getFlowerNeighbors() {
```

Part (b)

Write the move method for the Gardener class. A Gardener moves as follows:

- She checks her neighboring locations to determine if there are any flowers in neighboring locations.
- If there are flower neighbors, she will:
    - Choose one of the flowers at random.
    - Pick that flower (by having it remove itself from the grid).
    - Increment the number of flowers she has picked.
    - Move to a random, empty, neighboring location.
- If there are no neighboring flowers, she will move randomly into a neighboring location, removing whatever object (if any) is in that location.

In writing the move method, you may call getFlowerNeighbors; assume that getFlowerNeighbors works as specified.

Complete method move below:

```
/*
 * If there is at least one neighboring flower, pick a random
 * neighboring flower, increment the number of flowers picked, and
 * move into a random neighboring empty location.
 * Otherwise, move to a random neighboring location, removing
 * whatever object (if any) is in that location.
 */
public void move() {
```

Part (c)

Write the act method for the Gardener class. A Gardener acts as follows:

- The Gardener will go home (remove herself from her grid) if she has been gardening for more than 30 time steps (as recorded by her private steps field) or if she has been gardening for more than 10 time steps and the number of flowers she has picked is less than .1 times the number of time steps she has been gardening.

- If the Gardener does not go home, she will move (which includes picking a neighboring flower if there is one), and then increment the number of time steps she has been gardening.

In writing the act method, you may call getFlowerNeighbors and/or move; assume that those methods work as specified.

Complete method act below:

```
/*
 * If this gardener has been gardening for more than 30 time steps
 * or if she has been gardening for more than 10 time steps and the
 * number of flowers she has picked is less than .1 times the number of
 * time steps she has been gardening, then she will remove herself
 * from her grid.
 * Otherwise, she will move (which includes picking a neighboring
 * flower if there is one), then she will increment the number of
 * time steps she has been gardening.
 */
public void act() {
```

Question 2

Assume that a class called `BankAccount` has been implemented to represent one person's bank account. A partial declaration of the `BankAccount` class is given below.

```
public class BankAccount {

    private int accountNum;
    private double balance;

    // constructor not shown

    // returns the account number
    public int getAccountNum() { return accountNum; }

    // returns the current balance (how much money is in the account)
    public double getBalance() { return balance; }

    // adds the given amount to the current balance
    public void doDeposit(double amount) { balance += amount; }

    // subtracts the given amount from the current balance
    public void doWithdrawal(double amount) { balance -= amount; }
}
```

Part (a)

In order to process the various transactions performed at the bank (either by ATM or bank teller), a `Transaction` class is needed: A `Transaction` includes an account number (an integer), the transaction type (a string with a single character "d" for deposit or "w" for withdrawal), and the amount of the transaction (a double value for the amount to be deposited or withdrawn). Those values are assigned when the `Transaction` is created and can be accessed but not modified.

Write the complete class declaration for class `Transaction`. Include all necessary instance variables and implementations of its constructor and methods.

Part (b)

An `ATMTransaction` class (a subclass of `Transaction`) is also needed to represent one ATM transaction. In addition to the information in a `Transaction`, an `ATMTransaction` contains a string that represents the location of the ATM that was used. The value of that location is assigned when the `ATMTransaction` is created and can be accessed but not modified. Write a complete class declaration for the `ATMTransaction` class. Include all necessary instance variables and implementations of its constructor and methods.

Part (c)

A class Bank will be used to store information about all of the accounts in one bank, and to perform transactions on those accounts. An incomplete declaration of the Bank class is given below.

```
public class Bank {

    private BankAccount [] accounts;

    // precondition: accountNum is the number of an account in the
    //               accounts array.
    // postcondition: returns the index in the accounts array of
    //               the given account number.
    private int getIndex(int accountNum) { /* not shown */ }

    // precondition: trans is a transaction for an account in the
    //               accounts array.
    // postcondition: the account for trans has been modified to
    //               reflect the change specified by the transaction
    public void doOneTransaction(Transaction trans) { /* part (c) */ }
}
```

Write the doOneTransaction method of the Bank class, which has one Transaction parameter. Method doOneTransaction should find the BankAccount with the account number in the given Transaction, and it should deposit or withdraw the amount in the given Transaction from that account as appropriate.

For example, assume that accounts.length is four and that the elements in the array have the account numbers and balances shown below.

	[0]	[1]	[2]	[3]
account #:	100	107	102	105
balance:	100.27	57.30	150.00	5.25

Here are some examples to illustrate what the call oneTransaction(trans) should do.

Value of trans		**Modified element of** accounts **array**
accountNum:	107	[1]
transactionType:	"d"	107
amount:	10.50	67.80
accountNum:	100	[0]
transactionType:	"w"	100
amount:	100.27	0.0
accountNum:	105	[3]
transactionType:	"w"	105
amount:	6.00	-.75

In writing method doOneTransaction, you may include calls to method getIndex specified above in the declaration of the Bank class. You may also call the methods of the BankAccount and Transaction classes.

Complete method doOneTransaction below.

```
// precondition: trans is a transaction for an account in the
//               accounts array
// postcondition: the account for trans has been modified to
//               reflect the change specified by the transaction
public void doOneTransaction(Transaction trans) {
```

Question 3

Part (a)

Write method `numInArray`, as started below. `numInArray` should return the number of times the string s occurs in array A.

For example, assume that array A is as shown below.

```
[0]      [1]     [2]      [3]     [4]      [5]     [6]
"java"   "is"    "nice"   "so"    "nice"   "it"    "is"
```

Here are some examples of calls to method `numInArray`.

Method call	Returned value
numInArray(A, "java")	1
numInArray(A, "is")	2
numInArray(A, "nice")	2
numInArray(A, "ja")	0

Complete method `numInArray` below.

```
// postcondition: returns the number of times s occurs in A
public static int numInArray(String[] A, String s) {
```

Part (b)

Write method printAllNums, as started below. For every string s in array A, printAllNums should write (using System.out.println) the string s, followed by a colon and a space, then followed by the number of times that string occurs in array B.

For example, assume that arrays A and B are as shown below.

```
            [0]      [1]      [2]      [3]
    A:      "ice"   "cream"  "is"     "nice"


            [0]      [1]      [2]      [3]     [4]      [5]     [6]
    B:      "java"   "is"    "nice"   "so"    "nice"   "it"    "is"
```

The call printAllNums(A, B) should produce the following output:

```
ice: 0
cream: 0
is: 2
nice: 2
```

In writing printAllNums, you may include calls to method numInArray. Assume that numInArray works as specified.

Complete method printAllNums below.

```
// postcondition: for all k such that 0 <= k < A.length,
//                prints the string in A[k] followed by a colon
//                and a space and the number of times that string
//                occurs in B
public static void printAllNums( String[] A, String[] B ) {
```

Question 4

Assume that the Name class, which is partially defined below, is used to represent people's first names.

```
public class Name {
    private String myName;

    public Name( String S ) { myName = S; }  // constructor
    public int length() { return myName.length(); }
    public String prefix( int k ) { /* part (a) */ }
    public String suffix( int k ) { /* part (b) */ }
    public boolean isNickname( Name n ) { /* part (c) */ }
}
```

Part (a)

Write the prefix method of the Name class. The prefix method should return a string containing the first k characters in the name. If the name has fewer than k characters, the prefix method should return the entire string.

For example, assume that name N represents the name "Sandy". Below are some examples of calls to N's prefix method.

k	Result of the call N.prefix(k)
0	""
1	"S"
2	"Sa"
3	"San"
5	"Sandy"
6	"Sandy"

Complete method prefix below.

```
// precondition: k >= 0
// postcondition: returns a string containing the first k letters
//                in this name; if this name has fewer than k
//                letters, returns the whole name
public String prefix( int k ) {
```

Part (b)

Write the `suffix` method of the `Name` class. The `suffix` method should return a string containing the last `k` characters in the name. If the name has fewer than `k` characters, the `suffix` method should return the entire string.

For example, assume that name `N` represents the name `"Sandy"`. Below are some examples of calls to `N`'s `suffix` method.

k	Result of the call `N.suffix( k )`
0	`""`
1	`"y"`
2	`"dy"`
3	`"ndy"`
5	`"Sandy"`
6	`"Sandy"`

Complete method `suffix` below.

```
// precondition: k >= 0
// postcondition: returns a string containing the last k letters in
//                this name; if this name has fewer than k letters,
//                returns the whole name
public String suffix( int k ) {
```

Part (c)

Write the `isNickname` method of the `Name` class. The `isNickname` method should return `true` if and only if its parameter `nick` is made up of two parts:

1. A nonempty string that is a prefix of this name

2. The suffix `"ie"`

Below are some examples.

Name represented by N	Name represented by `nick`	Value returned by the call `N.isNickname( nick )`
Susan	Susie	true
David	Davie	true
Ann	Annie	true
Susan	Sus	false
Ann	Robbie	false
David	Davy	false

In writing method `isNickname`, you may include calls to methods `prefix` and `suffix`. Assume that both methods work as specified.

Complete method `isNickname` below.

```
// precondition: nick is not null
public boolean isNickname( Name nick ) {
```

Answers to Section I

1.	C	21.	E
2.	A	22.	A
3.	E	23.	B
4.	D	24.	D
5.	E	25.	D
6.	A	26.	E
7.	A	27.	A
8.	D	28.	C
9.	B	29.	C
10.	B	30.	D
11.	E	31.	D
12.	C	32.	B
13.	B	33.	A
14.	B	34.	D
15.	A	35.	A
16.	A	36.	B
17.	B	37.	B
18.	D	38.	E
19.	A	39.	C
20.	A	40.	C

Answers to Section II

Question 1
Part (a)

```
/*
 * Finds all neighboring locations that contain a flower
 * Precondition: This Gardener is in a Grid.
 * Postcondition: Returns an ArrayList containing the locations of
 *                all neighboring flowers.  If there are no flower
 *                neighbors, an empty ArrayList is returned.
 */
private ArrayList<Location> getFlowerNeighbors() {
    ArrayList<Location> flowers = new ArrayList<Location>();
    Grid<Actor> myGrid = getGrid();
    Location myLoc = getLocation();
    ArrayList<Location> allNeighboringLocs =
                        myGrid.getOccupiedAdjacentLocations(myLoc);
    for (Location loc : allNeighboringLocs) {
        Object neighbor = myGrid.get(loc);
        if (neighbor instanceof Flower) {
            flowers.add(loc);
        }
    }
    return flowers;
}
```

Part (b)

```
/*
 * If there is at least one neighboring flower, pick a random
 * neighboring flower, increment the number of flowers picked, and
 * move into a random neighboring empty location.
 * Otherwise, move to a random neighboring location, removing
 * whatever object (if any) is in that location.
 */
public void move() {
    ArrayList<Location> neighboringFlowers = getFlowerNeighbors();
    Location newLoc;
    Grid<Actor> myGrid = getGrid();
    Location myLoc = getLocation();
    ArrayList<Location> moveLocs;
    int r;
    if (neighboringFlowers.size() == 0) {
        moveLocs = myGrid.getValidAdjacentLocations(myLoc);
    } else {
```

```
        r = (int)(Math.random() * neighboringFlowers.size());
        Location flowerLoc = neighboringFlowers.get(r);
        Flower flower = (Flower)(myGrid.get(flowerLoc));
        flower.removeSelfFromGrid();
        flowersPicked++;
        moveLocs = myGrid.getEmptyAdjacentLocations(myLoc);
    }
    r = (int)(Math.random() * moveLocs.size());
    moveTo(moveLocs.get(r));
}
```

Part (c)

```
/*
 * If this gardener has been gardening for more than 30 time steps
 * or if she has been gardening for more than 10 time steps and the
 * number of flowers she has picked is less than .1 times the number
 * of time steps she has been gardening, then she will remove herself
 * from her grid.
 * Otherwise, she will move (which includes picking a neighboring
 * flower if there is one), then she will increment the number of
 * time steps she has been gardening.
 */
public void act() {
    if (steps > 30 ||
        (steps > 10 && flowersPicked < .1 * steps)) {
        removeSelfFromGrid();
    } else {
        move();
        steps++;
    }
}
```

Grading Guide

Part (a) getFlowerNeighbors   3 Points

+ 1/2   Retrieve the neighbors or occupied neighboring locations of the current location

+ 1   Loop over the neighbors or neighboring occupied locations

   + 1/2   attempt (must reference list in loop)

   + 1/2   correct

+ 1   Determine and store locations of neighboring flowers

   + 1/2   attempt to check neighbor to see if it is a flower

   + 1/2   correctly check neighbor and add its location to result list

+ 1/2   Correctly initialize result list and return it (must add to it during method)

Part (b) `move`   4 Points

+ 1/2   Call `getFlowerNeighbors`

+ 1/2   Correctly generate a random number to choose a flower neighbor

+ 2   Handle case where there is a flower neighbor (all pieces must be contained within a decision structure)

    + 1/2   choose an appropriate index from list of locations

    + 1/2   retrieve the flower at the chosen location and have it remove itself from the grid

    + 1/2   increment `flowersPicked`

    + 1/2   correctly choose a location to move to and move there

+ 1   Handle case where there is no flower neighbor

    + 1/2   retrieve neighboring locations and choose one at random

    + 1/2   appropriately call `moveTo`

Part (c) `act`   2 Points

+ 1   Decision

    + 1/2   attempt at decision (must have at least one part of the condition correct for attempt)

    + 1/2   correct decision

+ 1   Actions (need to be in correct place with respect to condition)

    + 1/2   remove the current object from the environment

    + 1/2   call `move` and increment the step count

Question 2

Part (a)

```
public class Transaction {

    private int accountNum;
    private String type;
    private double amount;

    public Transaction(int an, String t, double amt) {
        accountNum = an;
        type = t;
        amount = amt;
    }

    public int getAccountNum() { return accountNum; }
    public String getType() { return type; }
    public double getAmount() { return amount; }
}
```

Note: Points will be deducted if modifier methods (e.g., setAmount) are written.

Part (b)

```
public class ATMTransaction extends Transaction {

    private String location;

    public ATMTransaction(int an, String t, double amt, String loc) {
        super(an, t, amt);
        location = loc;
    }

    public String getLocation() { return location; }
}
```

Part (c)

```
public void doOneTransaction(Transaction trans) {
    int index = getIndex(trans.getAccountNum());
    if (trans.getType().equals("w"))
        accounts[index].doWithdrawal(trans.getAmount());
    else
        accounts[index].doDeposit(trans.getAmount());
}
```

Grading Guide

Part (a) The Transaction class   4 Points

+ 1   Private field declarations

+ 1   Constructor

    + 1/2   attempt (must include some parameters)

    + 1/2   correct

+1 1/2   Accessor methods

    + 1/2   attempt (must contain an attempt at methods for each variable)

    + 1   correct

+ 1/2   Absence of mutator methods

Part (b) The ATMTransaction class   3 Points

+ 1/2   Class header

+ 1/2   Private fields

+ 1   Constructor

    + 1/2   attempt (must include some parameters and a call to super)

    + 1/2   correct

+ 1   Accessor method for location

Part (c) doOneTransaction   2 Points

+ 1/2   Call to getIndex

+ 1   Determine transaction type

    + 1/2   attempt (must include a call to accessor method from part (a))

    + 1/2   correct

+ 1/2   Appropriate call to BankAccount method to perform the transaction

Question 3
Part (a)

```java
public static int numInArray(String[] A, String s) {
   int count = 0;

   for (String oneStr : A) {
      if (oneStr.equals(s)) count++;
   }
   return count;
}
```

Part (b)

```java
public static void printAllNums( String[] A, String[] B ) {
   for (String oneStr : A) {
      System.out.println(oneStr + ": " + numInArray(B, oneStr));
   }
}
```

Grading Guide

Part (a) numInArray   5 Points

+ 1   Initialize counter

+ 1   Loop over values in array

    + 1/2   attempt

    + 1/2   correct

+ 1   Compare against parameter

    + 1/2   attempt

    + 1/2   correct

+ 1   Increment counter in appropriate place

+ 1   Return counter

Part (b) printAllNums   4 Points

+ 1   Loop over values in A

    + 1/2   attempt

    + 1/2   correct

+ 1   Retrieve each individual value from A

+ 1   Call numInArray to check for number of occurrences

+ 1   Use System.out.println with value from A and count

Question 4

Part (a)

```
public String prefix( int k ) {
    if (myName.length() < k) return myName;
    else return myName.substring(0,k);
}
```

Part (b)

```
public String suffix( int k ) {
    int from;
    if (k > myName.length()) from = 0;
    else from = myName.length() - k;
    return myName.substring(from);
}
```

Part (c)

```
public boolean isNickname( Name n ) {
    if (!n.suffix(2).equals("ie")) return false;
    String pre1 = prefix(n.length() - 2);
    String pre2 = n.prefix(n.length() - 2);
    if (!pre1.equals(pre2)) return false;
    return true;
}
```

Grading Guide

Part (a) `prefix`   2 Points

+ 1/2   Check the length of the name

+ 1/2   Return the entire string when appropriate

+ 1   Return the appropriate substring

    + 1/2   attempt

    + 1/2   correct

Part (b) `suffix`   3 Points

+ 1/2   Check the length of the name

+ 1/2   Return the entire string when appropriate

+ 1   Return a string of the correct length

+ 1   Return the correct substring

Part (c) `isNickname`   4 Points

+2   Check for "ie" ending

    + 1/2   retrieve suffix

    + 1/2   attempt comparison (== ok for attempt)

    + 1/2   correct comparison

    + 1/2   return `false`

+ 1/2   Retrieve prefix of current name

+ 1/2   Retrieve prefix of parameter name

+ 1/2   Compare and return `true` if equal

+ 1/2   Return `false` otherwise

Practice Examination A-2

Section I

Time: 1 hour and 15 minutes
Number of questions: 40
Percent of total grade: 50

1. If addition had higher precedence than multiplication, then the value of the expression

    ```
    2 * 3 + 4 * 5
    ```

    would be which of the following?

    A. 14
    B. 26
    C. 50
    D. 70
    E. 120

2. Assume that x, y, and z are all int variables. Consider the following code segment:

    ```
    if (x == 0) {
       if (y == 1) z += 2;
    }
    else {
       z += 4;
    }
    System.out.print(z);
    ```

    What is printed if x, y, and z are all equal to zero before the code segment executes?

    A. 0
    B. 1
    C. 2
    D. 4
    E. 6

3. Consider the following instance variable and method:

```
private List<String> myList;

public void addList( List<String> L ) {
// add the items in L to myList
   for (String str : L) {
      myList.add(0, str);
   }
}
```

Assume that myList and L represent the lists shown below before method addList is called.

```
myList: [ A,  B,  C ]
L: [ X,  Y,  Z ]
```

Which of the following lists does myList represent when method addList returns?

A. [A, B, C, X, Y, Z]

B. [A, B, C, Z, Y, X]

C. [X, Y, Z, A, B, C]

D. [Z, Y, X, A, B, C]

E. [A, X, B, Y, C, Z]

4. Assume that arrays A and B both contain int values. Which of the following code segments returns true if and only if the kth elements of the two arrays are the same?

```
I.   return(A[k] == B[k]);
II.  if (A[k] == B[k]) {
        return true;
     }
     else return false;
III. if (A[k] == B[k]) {
        return true;
     }
     return false;
```

A. I only

B. II only

C. III only

D. II and III only

E. I, II, and III

5. Which of the following best describes what a class's constructor should do?

   A. Test all of the class's methods.

   B. Initialize the fields of this instance of the class.

   C. Determine and return the amount of storage needed by the fields of the class.

   D. Return to free storage all memory used by this instance of the class.

   E. Print a message informing the user that a new instance of this class has been created.

6. Consider designing an `Employee` interface that includes the following operations:

   - Return the number of hours worked this month.
   - Return the amount earned this month.
   - Raise the salary by a given amount.

   Which of the following is the best definition of the `Employee` interface?

   A.
   ```
   public interface Employee {
       private double hours;
       private double salary;
       double hoursWorked();
       double monthlyEarnings();
       void raiseSalary(double raise);
   }
   ```

   B.
   ```
   public interface Employee {
       private double hours;
       private double salary;
       double hoursWorked() { return hours; }
       double monthlyEarnings() { return hours * salary; }
       void raiseSalary(double raise) { salary += raise; }
   }
   ```

   C.
   ```
   public interface Employee {
       double hoursWorked();
       double monthlyEarnings();
       void raiseSalary( double raise );
   }
   ```

   D.
   ```
   public interface Employee {
       void hoursWorked();
       void monthlyEarnings();
       double raiseSalary(double raise);
   }
   ```

   E.
   ```
   public interface Employee {
       void hoursWorked() { hours = 40; }
       void monthlyEarnings() { earnings = 40 * salary; }
       double raiseSalary(double raise) { return salary+raise;}
   }
   ```

7. The code segment shown below was intended to set all of the elements on the diagonals of array A (a square array of ints) to 0 and to set the element in the middle of the array to 1. However, the code segment does not work as intended. (Line numbers are included for reference.)

```
1  // precondition: A is a nonempty, square array with
2  // an odd number of rows and columns
3  int size = A.length;
4  A[size/2][size/2] = 1;
5  for (int j=0; j<size; j++) A[j][j] = 0;
6  for (int j=0; j<size; j++) A[j][size-j-1] = 0;
```

When the code segment is tested, it is discovered that although the diagonal elements are set to 0, the middle element is also set to 0 instead of to 1. Which of the following changes fixes the code segment?

A. Swap lines 4 and 6.

B. Swap lines 5 and 6.

C. Swap lines 4 and 5.

D. Change line 3 to int size = A.length-1;.

E. Change line 4 to A[size/2+1][size/2+1] = 1;.

8. Consider the following instance variable and method:

```
private List<String> myList;

public boolean testList(String val) {
    for (String item : myList) {
        if (item.compareTo(val) > 0) return false;
    }
    return true;
}
```

Which of the following best describes the circumstances under which method testList returns true?

A. When no string in myList comes after val in lexicographic order

B. When no string in myList comes before val in lexicographic order

C. When no string in myList is the same as val

D. When all strings in myList are the same as val

E. When all strings in myList come before val in lexicographic order

Questions 9–11 rely on the following (incomplete) definition of the Book class:

```
public class Book {
    private double price;              // the price of this book

    public double getPrice() { ... } // returns the price of this book

    public static double totalPrice( Book[] inventory ) {
    // postcondition: returns the sum of the prices of the books in
    //                 the inventory array
       double sum = 0.0;
       for (int k=0; k<inventory.length; k++) {
          : missing code
       }
       return sum;
    }
}
```

9. Consider changing the Book class so that the price of a book can be set when a Book object is created. For example:

    ```
    Book b1 = new Book(10.50);  // price of b1 is $10.50
    Book b2 = new Book(25.00);  // price of b2 is $25.00
    ```

    Which of the following best describes the change that should be made?

    A. Define a constructor with no arguments.

    B. Define a constructor with one argument.

    C. Define a constructor with two arguments.

    D. Define a method named setPrice.

    E. It is not possible to change the Book class as specified.

10. Which of the following code segments could be used to replace *missing code* in method totalPrice so that it works as specified by its postcondition?

    A. sum += inventory.price[k];

    B. sum += inventory.getPrice(k);

    C. sum += inventory.Book[k];

    D. sum += inventory[k].Book();

    E. sum += inventory[k].getPrice();

11. Consider adding another method to the Book class with the following header:

```
public static double totalPrice( ArrayList<Book> inventory )
```

The new method would be the same as the existing `totalPrice` method except that its parameter, `inventory`, is an `ArrayList` of Books instead of an array of Books.

Which of the following statements about the proposed new method is true?

A. It is an example of inheritance.

B. It is an example of an interface.

C. It is an example of overloading.

D. It is an example of an abstract method.

E. It is an example of casting.

12. Consider the following code segment:

```
for (int j=0; j<M; j++) {
    for (int k=0; k<N; k++) {
        System.out.print("*");
    }
    System.out.println();
}
```

Assume that M and N are int variables, initialized to 2 and 3, respectively.
What is printed when the code segment executes?

A. ******

B. ***
    ***

C. **
    **
    **

D. ***
    **

E. **
    ***

13. Consider the incomplete method shown below.

```
public static int doSum(int start, int finish) {
// precondition: start <= finish
// postcondition returns the sum of the numbers from start to finish
   if ( start == finish ) return expression1;
   return expression2;
}
```

Which of the following could be used to replace *expression1* and *expression2* so that the method works as specified by its pre- and postconditions?

	expression1	*expression2*
A.	0	doSum(start+1, finish)
B.	0	doSum(start, finish-1)
C.	1	start + doSum(start, finish-1)
D.	start	doSum(start+1, finish)
E.	start	start + doSum(start+1, finish)

Questions 14 and 15 refer to the following information:

Assume that N and k are int variables and that A is an array of ints of length $N + 1$. Consider the following expression:

```
((k <= N) && (A[k] < 0)) || (A[k] == 0)
```

14. Under which of the following conditions must the expression evaluate to true?

A. A[k] is not equal to zero.

B. A[k] is equal to zero.

C. k is less than N.

D. k is less than or equal to N.

E. k is less than N, and A[k] is not equal to zero.

15. Recall that an out-of-bounds array index causes a runtime error. Which of the following statements is true?

A. Evaluating the expression will never cause a runtime error.

B. Evaluating the expression will cause a runtime error whenever A[k] is zero.

C. Evaluating the expression will cause a runtime error whenever A[k] is not zero.

D. Evaluating the expression will cause a runtime error whenever k is equal to N.

E. Evaluating the expression will cause a runtime error whenever k is greater than N.

Questions 16 and 17 refer to the following (incorrect) definitions of the `Car` and `SportsCar` classes (note that `SportsCar` is a subclass of `Car`).

```java
public class Car {
   private double price;
   private double milesPerGallon;
   private int daysSinceOilchange;

   // constructor
   public Car( double p, double mpg ) {
      price = p;
      milesPerGallon = mpg;
      daysSinceOilchange = 0;
   }

    public boolean needsOilchange() {
       return (daysSinceOilchange >= 90);
    }

    public void setDaysSinceOilchange(int days) {
       daysSinceOilchange = days;
    }

    public int getDaysSinceOilchange( ) {
       return daysSinceOilchange;
    }
 }


public class SportsCar extends Car {
   private int maxSpeed;

   // constructor
   public SportsCar(double p, double mpg, int max) {
      maxSpeed = max;
   }

   // override the needsOilchange method
   public boolean needsOilchange() {
      return (getDaysSinceOilchange() >= 30);
   }
}
```

16. The `SportsCar` constructor shown above does not compile. Which of the following correctly explains the error?

A. Parameters `p` and `mpg` are not used.

B. The order of the parameters is not correct.

C. The types of the left- and right-hand sides in the assignment to `maxSpeed` do not match.

D. The `price`, `milesPerGallon`, and `daysSinceOilchange` fields are not initialized.

E. There is no explicit call to the superclass constructor, and the superclass has no default (no-argument) constructor.

17. Assume that the `SportsCar` constructor has been defined correctly. Consider the following code segment:

```
Car myCar = new SportsCar(30000, 14.5, 120);
myCar.setDaysSinceOilchange(40);
if (myCar.needsOilchange()) System.out.println("Change oil");
else System.out.println("Do not change oil");
```

Which of the following statements about this code segment is true?

A. It will compile and run without error and will print `Change oil`.

B. It will compile and run without error and will print `Do not change oil`.

C. It will not compile because the type of `myCar` is `Car`, and the type of the value assigned to `myCar` is `SportsCar`.

D. It will not compile because `myCar` points to a `SportsCar`, and `SportsCar` has no `setDaysSinceOilchange` method.

E. It will compile, but there will be a runtime error when the second line is executed because `myCar` points to a `SportsCar`, and `SportsCar` has no `setDaysSinceOilchange` method.

18. Assume that A is a nonempty, rectangular, two-dimensional array of non-null objects. Consider the following method:

```
for (int j=0; j<A[0].length; j++) {
    if (! A[0][j].equals(A[A.length-1][j])) return false;
}
return true;
}
```

Which of the following best characterizes the conditions under which this code segment returns `true`?

A. Whenever the first and second rows of array A contain the same values

B. Whenever the first and last columns of array A contain the same values

C. Whenever the first and last rows of array A contain the same values

D. Whenever the first row and the first column of array A contain the same values

E. Whenever the first row and the last column of array A contain the same values

19. Consider the following code segment:

```
String[] firstArray, secondArray;
String s1, s2;
s1 = "cat";
s2 = "s" + s1;
firstArray = new String[3];
secondArray = firstArray;
firstArray[0] = s1;
firstArray[1] = s1;
firstArray[2] = s1;
secondArray[2] = s2;
s1 = "pig";
for (int k=0; k<3; k++) System.out.print(firstArray[k] + " ");
```

What happens when this code executes?

A. "cat cat cat" is printed.

B. "cat cat scat" is printed.

C. "pig pig pig" is printed.

D. Nothing is printed because the assignment to secondArray[2] causes an IndexOutOfBoundsException.

E. Nothing is printed because the assignment to secondArray[2] causes a NullPointer-Exception.

20. Assume that variable A is an array of ints. Consider the following incomplete code segment:

```
// postcondition: returns true if some value occurs more than
//                      once in A, false otherwise
   for (int j=0; j<A.length-1; j++) {
       statement
   }
return false;
```

Which of the following can be used to replace the placeholder *statement* so that the code segment works as specified by its postcondition?

A. `if (A[j] == A[j+1]) return true;`

B. `if (A[j] == A[A.length]) return true;`

C.
```
for (int k=0; k<A.length; k++) {
    if (A[j] == A[k]) return true;
}
```

D.
```
for (int k=j; k<A.length; k++) {
    if (A[j] == A[k]) return true;
}
```

E.
```
for (int k=j+1; k<A.length; k++) {
    if (A[j] == A[k]) return true;
}
```

Questions 21–24 involve reasoning about the GridWorld Case Study.

21. Which of the following methods of the `Grid` interface returns a data structure that might contain Bug objects?

   I. `getOccupiedLocations`
   II. `getOccupiedAdjacentLocations`
   III. `getNeighbors`

   A. I only

   B. II only

   C. III only

   D. I and II only

   E. I, II, and III

22. Which of the following statements about the inheritance structure of `Actor`, `Bug`, and `Flower` is true?

   A. `Bug` and `Flower` are both subclasses of `Actor`.

   B. `Bug` is a subclass of `Flower`.

   C. `Flower` is a subclass of `Bug`.

   D. `Actor` is a subclass of both `Bug` and `Flower`.

   E. `Actor` is a subclass of `Bug` only.

23. Assume that a method of the `Rock` class has a variable called `myBug` of type `Bug`. Including which of the following calls in the `Rock` class method would cause a compile-time error?

   A. `myBug.setColor(this.getColor())`

   B. `myBug.act()`

   C. `this.act()`

   D. `myBug.canMove()`

   E. `this.canMove()`

24. A new subclass of Bug called BlueBug is being defined. The BlueBug constructor should create a blue bug facing north. An incomplete version of the constructor is given below.

    ```
    public BlueBug() {
      <missing statements>
    }
    ```

    Which of the following is the best replacement for <missing statements> in the incomplete constructor?

    A. dir = 0;
    color = Color.BLUE;

    B. color = Color.BLUE;
    super();

    C. super();
    setDirection(0);

    D. super(Color.BLUE);

    E. super(Color.BLUE, 0);

25. Consider writing a program to be used to manage a collection of movies. There are three kinds of movies in the collection: dramas, comedies, and documentaries. The collector would like to keep track, for each movie, of its name, the name of the director, and the date when it was made. Some operations are to be implemented for all movies, and there will also be special operations for each of the three different kinds of movies. Which of the following is the best design?

    A. Define one class, Movie, with six fields: drama, comedy, documentary, name, director, and date.

    B. Define one superclass, Movie, with six subclasses: Drama, Comedy, Documentary, Name, Director, and Date.

    C. Define one superclass, Movie, with three fields: name, director, and date; and with three subclasses: Drama, Comedy, and Documentary.

    D. Define six unrelated classes: Drama, Comedy, Documentary, Name, Director, and Date.

    E. Define six classes: Drama, Comedy, Documentary, Name, Director, and Date. Make Date and Director subclasses of Name, and make Documentary and Comedy subclasses of Drama.

26. Assume that a method called `checkStr` has been written to determine whether a string is the same forward and backward. The following two sets of data are being considered to be used to test method `checkStr`:

Data Set 1	Data Set 2
"aba"	"abba"
"?"	"abab"
"z&*&z"	
"##"	

Which of the following is an advantage of data set 2 over data set 1?

  A. All strings in data set 2 have the same number of characters.

  B. Data set 2 contains a string for which method `checkStr` should return `false`, as well as a string for which method `checkStr` should return `true`.

  C. The strings in data set 2 contain only lowercase letters.

  D. Data set 2 contains fewer values than data set 1.

  E. Data set 2 has no advantage over data set 1.

Questions 27 and 28 refer to the following recursive method:

```
public static int compute(int x, int y) {
    if (x == y) return x;
    else return( compute(x+1, y-1) );
}
```

27. What is returned by the call `compute(1, 5)`?

  A. 1

  B. 2

  C. 3

  D. 4

  E. No value is returned because an infinite recursion occurs.

28. Which of the following calls leads to an infinite recursion?

  I.   `compute(2, 8)`
  II. `compute(8, 2)`
  III. `compute(2, 5)`

  A. I only

  B. II only

  C. III only

  D. I and II

  E. II and III

29. Three algorithms are being considered to look for a given value in an *unsorted* array of integers.

   Algorithm 1: Use binary search.

   Algorithm 2: Use sequential search.

   Algorithm 3: Sort the array, then use binary search.

   Which of the following statements about the three algorithms is true?

   A. All three will work; algorithm 1 will be most efficient.

   B. Only algorithms 1 and 2 will work; algorithm 1 will be most efficient.

   C. Only algorithms 1 and 3 will work; algorithm 1 will be most efficient.

   D. Only algorithms 2 and 3 will work; algorithm 2 will be most efficient.

   E. Only algorithms 2 and 3 will work; algorithm 3 will be most efficient.

30. Assume that the following interface and class have been defined:

```java
public interface Person {
   public String getName();
   public int getAge();
}


public class Student implements Person {
   private String name;
   private int age;

   //constructor
   public Student( String n, int a ) {
      name = n;
      age = a;
   }
   public String getName() { return name; }
   public int getAge() { return age; }
}
```

   Which of the following will cause a compile-time error?

   A. An attempt to create an instance of a `Person`

   B. An attempt to create an instance of a `Student`

   C. An attempt to define a method with a parameter of type `Person`

   D. An attempt to define a method with a parameter of type `Student`

   E. An attempt to define a subclass of the `Student` class

31. Which of the following best explains why a method might have the precondition N > 0?

    A. Every method must have a precondition or it will not compile.

    B. Including a precondition makes a method more efficient.

    C. Including the precondition ensures that if, when the method is called, variable N is *not* greater than 0, it will be set to 1 so that the precondition is satisfied.

    D. Including the precondition provides information to users of the method, specifying what is expected to be true whenever the method is called.

    E. This is an example of bottom-up design. The precondition is included to permit the method to be tested and debugged in isolation from the rest of the program. The precondition should be removed as soon as that phase of program development is complete.

Questions 32 and 33 concern the code segment shown below. The code segment was intended to count and return the number of values in *sorted* array A (which contains ints) that are smaller than the value in int variable x. However, the code segment sometimes causes an IndexOutOfBounds-Exception.

```
// precondition: A is sorted in ascending order.
int k = 0;
while ((A[k] < x) && (k < A.length)) k++;
return k;
```

32. Under what conditions does the code segment cause an IndexOutOfBoundsException?

    A. Always

    B. Whenever *no* values in array A are smaller than x

    C. Whenever *all* values in array A are smaller than x

    D. Whenever *some* value in array A is smaller than x

    E. Whenever *most* values in array A are smaller than x

33. Which of the following replacements for the while-loop condition would fix the code segment so that it works as intended?

    A. (A[k] < x) || (k < A.length)

    B. (A[k] < x) && (k <= A.length)

    C. (A[k] <= x) && (k < A.length)

    D. (k < A.length) || (A[k] < x)

    E. (k < A.length) && (A[k] < x)

34. Under which of the following conditions can a method be *overloaded;* that is, when can two methods with the same name be included in the same class?

   A. The methods do different things.

   B. The methods have different numbers or types of parameters.

   C. The methods have different parameter names.

   D. The methods have different preconditions.

   E. Two methods with the same name can never be included in the same class.

Questions 35 and 36 concern the following two ways to represent a set of integers (with no duplicates) with values in the range 0 to N:

  Method 1: Use an array of booleans of size $N+1$. The kth element of the array is `true` if k is in the set; otherwise, it is `false`.

  Method 2: Use an array of integers. The size of the array is the same as the current size of the set. Each element of the array holds one of the values that is in the set. The values are stored in the array in sorted order.

35. Assume that an `int` and a `boolean` require the same amount of space. Which of the following statements about the space requirements of the two methods is true?

   A. Method 1 requires less space than method 2 to represent an empty set.

   B. The amount of space required for method 1 is independent of the number of values in the set, whereas the amount of space required for method 2 varies depending on the number of values in the set.

   C. The amount of space required for method 2 is independent of the number of values in the set, whereas the amount of space required for method 1 varies depending on the number of values in the set.

   D. The amount of space required for both method 1 and method 2 is independent of the number of values in the set.

   E. The amount of space required for both method 1 and method 2 varies depending on the number of values in the set.

36. Which of the following operations can be implemented more efficiently using method 1 rather than using method 2?

   I.   Determine whether a given value is in the set.
   II. Remove a given value from the set.
   III. Print all of the values in the set.

   A. I only

   B. II only

   C. III only

   D. I and II only

   E. I, II, and III

37. Two programmers are working together to write a program. One is implementing a List class and the other is writing code that includes variables of type List. The programmers have decided that the List class will include a public method named search. Which of the following facts about the search method does *not* need to be agreed on by both programmers?

A. The names of the parameters

B. The number of parameters

C. The pre- and postconditions

D. The type of each parameter

E. The return type

38. Consider the following recursive method. (Assume that method readInt reads one integer value typed in by the user.)

```
public static void print(int n) {
    int x;
    if (n > 0) {
        x = readInt();
        if (x > 0) {
            print(n-1);
            System.out.println(x);
        }
        else print(n);
    }
}
```

Which of the following best describes what happens as a result of the call print(5)?

A. The first five numbers typed by the user are printed in the order in which they are typed.

B. The first five numbers typed by the user are printed in the opposite order to that in which they are typed.

C. The first five positive numbers typed by the user are printed in the order in which they are typed.

D. The first five positive numbers typed by the user are printed in the opposite order to that in which they are typed.

E. Nothing is printed because the call causes an infinite recursion.

39. Consider the following code segment:

```
x = y;
y = !x;
x = !y;
```

Assume that x and y are initialized boolean variables. Which of the following statements is true?

A. The final value of x is the same as the initial value of x.

B. The final value of x is the same as the initial value of y.

C. The final value of y is the same as the initial value of y.

D. The final value of y is the same as the initial value of x.

E. It is not possible to say anything about the final values of x and y without knowing their initial values.

40. Assume that a class includes the following instance variables and methods:

```
private double[] dblList;
private int[] intList;

public boolean search(double d) {
// search version 1
   for (oneDbl : dblList) {
      if (d == oneDbl) return true;
   }
   return false;
}

public boolean search(int n) {
// search version 2
   for (int oneInt : intList) {
      if (n == oneInt) return true;
   }
   return false;
}

public void test() {
   if (search(5.5)) System.out.println("found!");
}
```

Which of the following statements about this code is true?

A. It will not compile because the class includes two methods named `search`.

B. It will not compile because the class does not include a version of the `search` method that matches the call in method `test`.

C. It will compile. When method `test` is called, if `dblList` is not null, version 1 of the `search` method will be called; if `dblList` is null, version 2 of the `search` method will be called.

D. It will compile. When method `test` is called, version 1 of the `search` method will be called.

E. It will compile. When method `test` is called, version 2 of the `search` method will be called.

Section II

Time: 1 hour and 45 minutes
Number of questions: 4
Percent of total grade: 50

Question 1

This question involves reasoning about the code from the GridWorld Case Study.

Consider three new classes:

1. A new subclass of Actor, called Food, that represents edible objects in a grid.
2. A new implementation of the Grid interface, called FoodGrid, that provides a list of the locations containing food.
3. A new subclass of Critter, called EatingCritter, that eats all neighboring food objects, then moves toward a randomly chosen remaining food object if there is one.

Assume that the FoodGrid class includes the following method.

```
public ArrayList<Location> getFoodLocations()
// returns a list of the locations in this grid that contain food;
// the list is empty if there are no locations that contain food
```

An EatingCritter's methods should work as follows:

getActors(): Get a list of all neighboring actors.

processActors(ArrayList<Actor> actors): Eat all food actors in list actors (by having them remove themselves from the grid).

getMoveLocations(): Get a list of all neighboring locations that are in the direction of a food actor.

selectMoveLocation(ArrayList<Location> locs): If locs is empty, return the current location. Otherwise, select and return a randomly chosen location in locs.

makeMove(Location loc): Move to location loc.

act(): Call getActors to get a list of all neighboring actors; pass that list to processActors, which will process them; call getMoveLocations to get a list of locations to move to; and pass that list to makeMove to make the chosen move.

Part (a)

Which of the `Critter` methods must be over ridden in order to correctly implement the `EatingCritter` class? Circle the correct answer(s).

```
act                 getActors              processActors

getMoveLocations  selectMoveLocation  makeMove
```

Part (b)

Write the `EatingCritter` method `getMoveLocations`. The `getMoveLocations` method should return a list of the neighboring locations that are in the direction of a food actor. If there are no food actors in the grid, the method should return an empty list.

In writing the `getMoveLocations` method, you should make the following assumptions:

- The critter is in a `FoodGrid`.
- Neither the critter's current location nor any of its neighboring locations contain food.

Complete method `getMoveLocations` below:

```
public ArrayList<Location> getMoveLocations() {
```

Question 2

Consider a hierarchy of classes used by a power company to keep track of the buildings where they supply electricity. The hierarchy is represented by the following diagram:

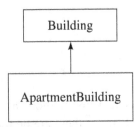

Note that an `ApartmentBuilding` is a subclass of `Building`.

A building is represented by the class defined below.

```java
public class Building {
    public static final double RATE = 3.25;
    private String address;
    private double wattHours;   // units of electricity used in 1 month

    public Building(String ad) {
        address = ad;
        wattHours = 0;
    }

    // returns the amount owed by this building
    public double amtOwed( ) { /* not shown */ }

    // other methods not shown
}
```

Part (a)

An `ApartmentBuilding` is different from a regular building because instead of keeping track of the watt hours used for the whole building, it needs to keep track of the watt hours used by each of the individual apartments in the building.

Write a complete declaration of class `ApartmentBuilding` including the following:

- A private instance variable (an array) to be used to store the apartments' watt hours.
- A constructor with two parameters: the address of the apartment building and the number of apartments. The constructor should initialize the building's address field as well as initializing the array to be big enough to store watt hours for each apartment in the building.
- An implementation of `amtOwed` that returns the amount of money owed by the entire building for the electricity used (calculated by multiplying the sum of the `wattHours` for the entire building by the `RATE`).

Write the complete `ApartmentBuilding` class declaration.

Part (b)

Consider the following partial declaration for the ServiceArea class. A ServiceArea represents an entire area being served by this power company.

```
public class ServiceArea {

    private ArrayList<Building> allBuildings;  // a list of Buildings

    public ServiceArea() { /* constructor not shown */ }

    public double totalSales() { /* part (b) */ }

    // other methods not shown
}
```

Write the totalSales method of class ServiceArea. The method should return the total amount of money owed by all of the buildings in the allBuildings list. Assume that the buildings' amtOwed methods work correctly regardless of what you wrote for part (a).

Complete method totalSales below.

```
public double totalSales() {
```

Question 3

This question concerns the two classes, Product and GroceryStore, partially defined below.

```java
public class Product {
    private String name;
    private int numInStock;

    // constructor not shown
    public String getName() { return name; }
    public int getNumInStock() { return numInStock; }
    public void sellOne() { numInStock--; }
}

public class GroceryStore {
    private Product[] stock;

    // constructor not shown

    // precondition: no two Products in the stock array have the
    //               same name
    // postcondition: carries out the sale of the named product if
    //                possible and returns true or false depending
    //                on whether the sale is successful
    public boolean oneSale(String name) {
        /* part (b) */
    }

    // precondition: no two Products in the stock array have the
    //               same name
    // postcondition: attempts to carry out a sale for each name
    //                in the orders array, creating and returning
    //                an ArrayList containing the names of all
    //                products for which a sale is not successful
    public ArrayList<String> allSales(String[] orders) {
        /* part (c) */
    }

    // precondition: no two Products in the stock array have the
    //               same name
    // postcondition: returns the index of the Product in the stock
    //                array with the given name, or -1 if there is
    //                no such Product in the array
    private int findItem(String name) {
        /* part (a) */
    }
}
```

Part (a)

Write the findItem method of the GroceryStore class. As specified by its postcondition, findItem should return the index of the Product in the stock array with the given name, or it should return −1 if there is no such Product in the array.

Complete method findItem below.

```
// precondition: no two Products in the stock array have the
//               same name
// postcondition: returns the index of the Product in the stock array
//               with the given name, or returns -1 if there is no
//               such Product in the array
private int findItem(String name) {
```

Part (b)

Write the oneSale method of the GroceryStore class. Method oneSale has one parameter: the name of one product (that a customer would like to buy). Method oneSale should attempt to carry out the sale of the named product, and it should return true or false depending on whether the sale is successful. The sale is successful if there is a product in the stock array with the given name and if the number of items in stock of that product is greater than zero. In that case, oneSale should subtract one from the number of items in stock and return true. If there is no product in the stock array with the given name or if the number of items in stock for that product is less than or equal to zero, oneSale should return false.

For example, assume that stock.length is four and that the elements in the array are as shown below.

	[0]	[1]	[2]	[3]
name:	"milk"	"eggs"	"butter"	"coffee"
numInStock:	20	3	0	1

If oneSale is called with the name "eggs", it should subtract one from the number of eggs in stock and return true. If oneSale is called with the name "juice", it should return false (because there is no juice in the stock array). If oneSale is called with the name "butter", it should return false (because there are no butter items currently in stock).

In writing method oneSale, you may include calls to method findItem. Assume that findItem works correctly, regardless of what you wrote for part (a).

Complete method oneSale below.

```
// precondition: no two Products in the stock array have the
//               same name
// postcondition: carries out the sale of the named product if
//               possible and returns true or false depending
//               on whether the sale is successful
public boolean oneSale(String name) {
```

Part (c)

Write the `allSales` method of the `GroceryStore` class. Method `allSales` has one parameter: an array of product names called `orders`. For each name in the `orders` array, `allSales` should attempt to carry out the sale of the named product. It should create a new `ArrayList` containing the names of all products for which a sale is not successful (a product name should appear more than once in the new `ArrayList` if there is more than one failing sale of that product). Finally, it should return the new `ArrayList`.

For example, assume that the `stock` array is initially as shown in part (b). Also assume that `allSales` is called with the array of names:

[0]	[1]	[2]	[3]	[4]	[5]	[6]	[7]	[8]
"eggs"	"milk"	"milk"	"butter"	"coffee"	"tea"	"coffee"	"milk"	"coffee"

Method `allSales` should carry out five successful sales (eggs, milk, milk, coffee, milk), changing the appropriate `Products` in the `stock` array. It should create and return a new `ArrayList` containing the strings

```
"butter" "tea" "coffee" "coffee"
```

because the number of butter items is initially zero, there is no tea product, and the number of coffee items is zero when the second and third attempts to sell one coffee item are made.

In writing method `allSales`, you may include calls to method `oneSale`. Assume that `oneSale` works correctly, regardless of what you wrote for part (b).

Complete method `allSales` below.

```
// precondition: no two Products in the stock array have the
//               same name
// postcondition: attempts to carry out a sale for each name in the
//                orders array, creating and returning an ArrayList
//                containing the names of all products for which a
//                sale is not successful
public ArrayList<String> allSales(String[] orders) {
```

Question 4

A restaurant uses a class called `Table` to keep track of the orders placed by the diners at one table. An order includes a `String` (the food being ordered) and a `Double` (the price of the order). A declaration of the `Table` class is given below.

```
public class Table {
    private ArrayList<String> foods;  // a list of Strings, one for each person
                                      // at this table
    private ArrayList<Double> prices; // a list of Doubles, one for each
                                      // person at this table

    // constructor
    public Table() {
        foods = new ArrayList<String>();
        prices = new ArrayList<Double>();
    }

    public void placeOrder(String food, Double price) {
        foods.add(food);
        prices.add(price);
    }

    public ArrayList<String> getFoods() { return foods; }

    public ArrayList<Double> getPrices() { return prices; }
}
```

A `RestaurantTables` class is used to represent all of the tables in the restaurant, and to place orders and compute bills and tips for each table. A partial declaration of the `RestaurantTables` class is given below.

```
public class RestaurantTables {

    private Table[] allTables;  // one element in the array for each
                                // table in the restaurant

    // constructor not shown

    // precondition: 0 <= tableNum < allTables.length, and
    //               foods.length == prices.length
    // postcondition: all of the foods and prices in the two parameters
    //                have been added to the orders for allTables[tableNum]
    public void placeTableOrders(int tableNum, String[] foods,
                                 double[] prices) {
        /* part (a) */
    }
```

```
// precondition: 0 <= tableNum < allTables.length
// postcondition: returns an ArrayList of Double values: the prices
//                  for the orders at the given table
private ArrayList<Double> tableOrderPrices(int tableNum) {
    return allTables[tableNum].getPrices();
}


// precondition: 0 <= tableNum < allTables.length
// postcondition: returns the total bill for table tableNum
//                  (the sum of the prices of the orders)
public double totalBill(int tableNum) { /* part (b) */ }


// precondition: 0 <= tableNum < allTables.length
// postcondition: returns the tip for table tableNum: 15% of the total
//                  bill if there are 6 or more orders for table tableNum;
//                  0 otherwise.
public double computeTip(int tableNum) { /* part (c) */ }
}
```

Part (a)

Write method `placeTableOrders`. Method `placeTableOrders` should place the orders represented by its two array parameters for table `tableNum`.

Complete method `placeTableOrders` below.

```
// precondition: 0 <= tableNum < allTables.length, and
//                  foods.length == prices.length
// postcondition: all of the foods and prices in the two parameters
//                  have been added to the orders for allTables[tableNum]
public void placeTableOrders(int tableNum, String[] foods,
                             double[] prices) {
```

Part (b)

Write method `totalBill`. Method `totalBill` should compute and return the bill for table `tableNum` (the sum of the prices for the orders placed by that table).

Complete method `totalBill` below.

```
// precondition: 0 <= tableNum < allTables.length
// postcondition: returns the total bill for table tableNum
//                  (the sum of the prices of the orders)
public double totalBill(int tableNum) {
```

Part (c)

Write method `computeTip`. Method `computeTip` should return 15% of the total bill if there are six or more orders from the table; otherwise, it should return 0.

Complete method `computeTip` below.

```
// precondition: 0 <= tableNum < allTables.length
// postcondition: returns the tip for table tableNum: 15% of the total
//                bill if there are 6 or more orders for table tableNum;
//                0.0 otherwise.
public double computeTip(int tableNum) {
```

Answers to Section I

1.	D	21.	C
2.	A	22.	A
3.	D	23.	E
4.	E	24.	D
5.	B	25.	C
6.	C	26.	B
7.	A	27.	C
8.	A	28.	E
9.	B	29.	D
10.	E	30.	A
11.	C	31.	D
12.	B	32.	C
13.	E	33.	E
14.	B	34.	B
15.	E	35.	B
16.	E	36.	D
17.	A	37.	A
18.	C	38.	D
19.	B	39.	B
20.	E	40.	D

Answers to Section II

Question 1
Part (a)

act   getActors   ┌─────────────────┐
                                         │ processActors   │
                                         └─────────────────┘
┌───────────────────┐
│ getMoveLocations │   selectMoveLocation   makeMove
└───────────────────┘

Part (b)

```
public ArrayList<Location> getMoveLocations() {
    // get all locations containing food
    // for each, get the direction from this critter toward that location
    // get the neighboring location in that direction
    // include that neighboring location in the list to be returned
    FoodGrid<Actor> myGrid = (FoodGrid)getGrid();
    Location myLoc = getLocation();
    ArrayList<Location> moveLocations = new ArrayList<Location>();
    ArrayList<Location> foodLocs = myGrid.getFoodLocations();
    for (Location targetLoc : foodLocs) {
        int dir = myLoc.getDirectionToward(targetLoc);
        Location moveLoc = myLoc.getAdjacentLocation(dir);
        if (! moveLocations.contains(moveLoc)) {
            moveLocations.add(moveLoc);
        }
    }
    return moveLocations;
}
```

Grading Guide

Part (a) Methods to be over ridden   4 points

+ 2   One point for each method correctly circled

+ 2   One-half point for each method not mistakenly circled

Part (b) getMoveLocations   5 points

+ 1/2   Retrieve the locations containing food

+ 1   Loop over the food locations

    + 1/2   attempt (must reference list in loop)

    + 1/2   correct

+1 1/2   Determine direction toward a food location

+1 1/2   Determine neighboring location in that direction

+ 1/2   Correctly initialize result list and return it (must add to it during method)

Question 2
Part (a)

```
public class ApartmentBuilding extends Building {

    private double [] wattHours;

    public ApartmentBuilding(String ad, int numUnits) {
        super(ad);
        wattHours = new double[numUnits];
    }

    public double amtOwed() {
        double sum = 0;
        for (double hrs : wattHours) {
            sum += hrs;
        }
        return sum*RATE;
    }
}
```

Part (b)

```
public double totalSales() {
    double sum = 0;
    for (Building oneBldg : allBuildings) {
        sum += oneBldg.amtOwed();
    }
    return sum;
}
```

Grading Guide

Part (a) The `ApartmentBuilding` class   6 Points

+ 1   Class declaration (must extend `Building`)

+ 1   Private field declaration (array should not be initialized)

+ 2   Constructor

> + ½   method header attempt
>
> + ½   call to super attempt
>
> + ½   initialization of array attempt (must include passed parameter)
>
> + ½   correct

+ 2   `amtOwed`

> + ½   initialize sum
>
> + ½   loop
>
> + ½   update of sum
>
> + ½   return sum

Part (b) `totalSales`   3 Points

+ ½   Initialization of sum

+ 1   Loop (correct point only)

+ 1   Update of sum

> + ½   attempt (must reference `allBuildings`)
>
> + ½   correct (must include correct call to `amtOwed`)

+ ½   Return sum

Question 3
Part (a)

```java
private int findItem(String name) {
    for (Product oneProd : stock) {
        if (oneProd.getName().equals(name)) return k;
    }
    return -1;
}
```

Part (b)

```java
public boolean oneSale(String name) {
    int k = findItem(name);
    if (k == -1) return false;
    if (stock[k].getNumInStock() <= 0) return false;
    stock[k].sellOne();
    return true;
}
```

Part (c)

```java
public ArrayList<String> allSales(String[] orders) {
    ArrayList<String> L = new ArrayList<String>();
    for (String oneOrder : orders) {
        if (!oneSale(oneOrder)) {
            L.add(oneOrder);
        }
    }
    return L;
}
```

Grading Guide

Part (a) findItem   3 Points

+ 1   Loop over stock array

    + 1/2   attempt (must reference stock within the loop)

    + 1/2   correct

+ 1   Compare the name in the array to parameter

    + 1/2   attempt

    + 1/2   correct

+ 1   Return appropriate values

    + 1/2   return index from loop

    + 1/2   return −1

Part (b) oneSale   3 Points

+ 1   Call findItem

+ 1   Comparison for appropriate stock

    + 1/2   attempt (must include either check for not found (−1) or numInStock < 0)

    + 1/2   correct

+ 1/2 Sell one

+ 1/2 Appropriate return

Part (c) allSales   3 Points

+ 1   ArrayList

    + 1/2   creation of ArrayList

    + 1/2   return of ArrayList

+ 1   Loop over orders array

    + 1/2   attempt (must reference orders within loop)

    + 1/2   correct

+ 1/2 Call to oneSale with test for success

+ 1/2 Add value to the ArrayList

Question 4
Part (a)

```
public void placeTableOrders(int tableNum, String[] foods,
                             double[] prices) {
   for (int i=0; i<foods.length; i++) {
      allTables[tableNum].placeOrder(foods[i], prices[i]);
   }
}
```

Part (b)

```
public double totalBill(int tableNum) {
   ArrayList<Double> prices = allTables[tableNum].getPrices();
   double total = 0;

   for (Double onePrice : prices) {
      total += onePrice.doubleValue();
   }

   return total;
}
```

Part (c)

```
public double computeTip(int tableNum) {
   ArrayList<Double> prices = allTables[tableNum].getPrices();
   if (prices.size() < 6) return 0;
   return .15 * totalBill(tableNum);
}
```

Grading Guide

Part (a) `placeTableOrders`   2 Points

+ 1   Loop over foods or prices

    + 1/2   attempt (must reference foods and prices in body)

    + 1/2   correct

+ 1   Correctly add orders

    + 1/2   attempt (must call `placeOrder`)

    + 1/2   correct

Part (b) `totalBill`   4 Points

+ 1   Get list of prices for table `tableNum`

    + 1/2   attempt

    + 1/2   correct

+ 1   Loop over prices

    + 1/2   attempt

    + 1/2   correct (must reference `ArrayList` in body)

+ 1   Add the values of prices to the total

+ 1   Create and return the sum

    + 1/2   create variable to store the sum

    + 1/2   return calculated value

Part (c) `computeTip`   3 Points

+1 1/2   Determine number of orders

    + 1/2   attempt

    + 1   correct

+ 1   Return tip if >= 6 orders

    + 1/2   attempt (must include call to `totalBill`)

    + 1/2   correct

+ 1/2   Return 0 if < 6 orders

Practice Examination A-3

Section I

Time: 1 hour and 15 minutes
Number of questions: 40
Percent of total grade: 50

1. Which of the following statements about Java variables and parameters is true?

   A. A variable must be declared before it is used.

   B. The same variable name cannot be used in two different methods.

   C. Variables used as indexes in *for-loops* must be named i, j, or k.

   D. It is good programming practice to use single letters as the names of all variables.

   E. It is good programming practice to name formal parameters param1, param2, and so on, so that it is clear where they appear in the method's list of parameters.

2. The expression

   ```
   (x && !y)
   ```

   is equivalent to which of the following expressions?

   A. (x || !y)

   B. (!x || y)

   C. !(!x || y)

   D. (!x && y)

   E. !(!x && y)

3. Which of the following is *not* an example of a good use of comments?

   A. Comments included at the beginning of a method to specify the method's pre- and postconditions

   B. Comments included at the end of every line of a method to explain what that line of code does

   C. Comments included at the beginning of a method to say which of the class's fields are modified by that method

   D. Comments included in a class's constructor to explain how the class object is initialized

   E. Comments included before a loop to say what is true each time the loop is executed

4. Assume that variable A is an array of Objects and variable ob is an Object. Consider the following two expressions:

    Expression 1: (A[k].equals(ob)) && (A[k] != null)

    Expression 2: (A[k] != null) && (A[k].equals(ob))

    Which of the following statements about these two expressions is true?

    A. If ob is null, expression 1 will cause a NullPointerException and expression 2 will not cause that exception.

    B. If ob is null, both expression 1 and expression 2 will cause a NullPointerException.

    C. If A[k] is null, expression 1 will cause a NullPointerException and expression 2 will not cause that exception.

    D. If A[k] is null, expression 2 will cause a NullPointerException and expression 1 will not cause that exception.

    E. If A[k] is null, both expression 1 and expression 2 will cause a NullPointerException.

5. Consider the following code segment; assume that A is an array of doubles, and that val is a double.

    ```
    boolean tmp=false;
    for (double d : A) {
        tmp = (d == val);
    }
    return tmp;
    ```

    Which of the following best characterizes the conditions under which this code segment returns true?

    A. Whenever array A contains value val

    B. Whenever the first element of array A has value val

    C. Whenever the last element of array A has value val

    D. Whenever more than one element of array A has value val

    E. Whenever exactly one element of array A has value val

6. Consider writing a program to be used to manage information about the animals on a farm. The farm has three kinds of animals: cows, pigs, and goats. The cows are used to produce both milk and meat. The goats are used only to produce milk, and the pigs are used only to produce meat.

Assume that an `Animal` class has been defined. Which of the following is the best way to represent the remaining data?

A. Define two subclasses of the `Animal` class: `MilkProducer` and `MeatProducer`. Define two subclasses of the `MilkProducer` class: `Cow` and `Goat`; and define two subclasses of the `MeatProducer` class: `Cow` and `Pig`.

B. Define three subclasses of the `Animal` class: `Cow`, `Goat`, and `Pig`. Also define two interfaces: `MilkProducer` and `MeatProducer`. Define the `Cow` and `Goat` classes to implement the `MilkProducer` interface, and define the `Cow` and `Pig` classes to implement the `MeatProducer` interface.

C. Define five new classes, not related to the `Animal` class: `Cow`, `Goat`, `Pig`, `MilkProducer`, and `MeatProducer`.

D. Define five subclasses of the `Animal` class: `Cow`, `Goat`, `Pig`, `MilkProducer`, and `MeatProducer`.

E. Define two subclasses of the `Animal` class: `MilkProducer` and `MeatProducer`. Also define three interfaces: `Cow`, `Goat`, and `Pig`. Define the `MilkProducer` class to implement the `Cow` and `Goat` interfaces, and define the `MeatProducer` class to implement the `Cow` and `Pig` interfaces.

Questions 7–9 refer to the following incomplete definitions of the Book and TextBook classes (note that TextBook is a subclass of Book).

```java
public class Book {
    private String name;
    private double price;

    // constructor
    public Book( String n, double p ) {
        name = n;
        price = p;
        System.out.println("created a book");
    }

    public static Book cheapestBook( Book[] bookList ) {
    // precondition: bookList.length > 0
    // return the book with the lowest price
        : missing code
    }
}


public class TextBook extends Book {
    private String classUsedIn;

    // constructor
    public TextBook( String n, double p, String class ) {
        super(n, p);
        classUsedIn = class;
        System.out.println("created a textbook");
    }

    public static TextBook getBookForClass(String className,
                                       TextBook[] textbookList) {
    // return the first textbook in textbookList that is used in the given
    // class (or null if there is no such textbook)
        : missing code
    }
}
```

7. Assume that the following declarations have been made:

   ```
   Book b;
   Book[] B;
   TextBook tb;
   TextBook[] TB;
   ```

   and that all four variables have been properly initialized. Which of the following statements will *not* compile?

   A. `b = Book.cheapestBook(B);`

   B. `b = Book.cheapestBook(TB);`

   C. `b = TextBook.getBookForClass("Intro to Java", TB);`

   D. `tb = TextBook.getBookForClass("Intro to Java", B);`

   E. `tb = TextBook.getBookForClass("Intro to Java", TB);`

8. Note that methods `cheapestBook` and `getBookForClass` are declared *static*. Which of the following statements is true?

   A. It is appropriate for the two methods to be static because they both operate on arrays passed as parameters rather than on fields of the two classes.

   B. Although the code works as is, because the two methods return single objects rather than arrays, they really shouldn't be declared static.

   C. It is appropriate for the `cheapestBook` method to be either static or non static, but because `TextBook` is a subclass of `Book`, the `getBookForClass` method must be static if the `cheapestBook` method is static.

   D. Because the two methods are static, the *missing code* for the method bodies cannot contain any recursive calls.

   E. It is appropriate for the two methods to be static, but if they had return type `void` they could not be static.

9. Consider the following declaration and initialization:

   ```
   Book oneBook = new TextBook("ABC", 10.50, "kindergarten");
   ```

   Which of the following statements about this code is true?

   A. The code will not compile because the type of the left-hand side of the assignment is `Book`, and the type of the right-hand side is `TextBook`.

   B. The code will compile, but there will be a runtime error when it is executed because the type of the left-hand side of the assignment is `Book`, and the type of the right-hand side is `TextBook`.

   C. The code will compile and execute without error; only `created a book` will be printed.

   D. The code will compile and execute without error; only `created a textbook` will be printed.

   E. The code will compile and execute without error, and both `created a book` and `created a textbook` will be printed.

10. Consider the following definitions of the `Baseclass` and `Subclass` classes.

```
public class Baseclass {
   private int myInt;
   private String myString;

   // constructor
   public Baseclass( ) {
      myInt = 0;
      myString = "";
   }

   // other methods not shown
}

public class Subclass extends Baseclass {
   private double myDouble;

   // constructor
   public Subclass(int anInt, String aString, double aDouble) {
      myInt = anInt;
      myString = aString;
   }

   // other methods not shown
}
```

The `Subclass` constructor shown above does not compile. Which of the following correctly explains the error?

A. The superclass constructor has no arguments, so the `Subclass` constructor cannot have any arguments, either.

B. Fields `myInt` and `myString` are *private* fields of `Baseclass`, so they cannot be assigned to in the `Subclass` constructor.

C. There is no call to the superclass constructor.

D. Parameter `aDouble` is not used.

E. The `myDouble` field is not initialized.

11. Consider the following instance variable and method.

```
private List<String> L;

public String[][] makeArray() {
    // precondition: L.size() > 0
    int num = L.size();
    int n = (int)Math.sqrt(num);
    String[][] result = new String[n][n];
    for (int j=0; j<n; j++) {
        for (int k=0; k<n; k++) {
            num--;
            result[j][k] = L.get(num);
        }
    }
    return result;
}
```

If L represents the list

```
[ "a", "b", "c", "d" ]
```

which of the following would be the value returned by a call to makeArray?

A. | "a" | "b" | "c" | "d" |

B. | "d" | "c" | "b" | "a" |

C. | "a" | "d" | "b" | "c" |

D.
| "a" | "b" |
| "c" | "d" |

E.
| "d" | "c" |
| "b" | "a" |

12. Consider the following code segment:

```
ArrayList<Integer> L = new ArrayList<Integer>();
int k = 0;
while (k<11) {
   L.add(new Integer(k));
   k++;
}
k = 0;
while (k<L.size()) {
   L.remove(k);
   k++;
}
for (k=0; k<L.size(); k++) {
   System.out.print(L.get(k) + " ");
}
```

What happens when this code executes?

A. The second *while-loop* causes an `IndexOutOfBoundsException`.

B. The *for-loop* causes an `IndexOutOfBoundsException`.

C. There is no exception, but nothing is printed because the list is empty after the second *while-loop*.

D. There is no exception; 1 3 5 7 9 is printed.

E. There is no exception; 6 7 8 9 10 is printed.

13. Assume that variable A is an array of *N* integers and that the following assertion is true:

```
A[0] != A[k] for all k such that 1 <= k < N
```

Which of the following is a valid conclusion?

A. Array A is sorted.

B. Array A is not sorted.

C. Array A contains no duplicates.

D. The value in A[0] is the smallest value in the array.

E. The value in A[0] does not occur anywhere else in the array.

14. Assume that variable `A` is an `ArrayList<String>` of size five. Consider the following code segment:

```
int N = A.size();
for (int k=0; k<=N/2; k++) {
   A.set(k, "X");
   A.set(N-k-1, "O");
}
```

Which of the following correctly illustrates `A` after the code segment executes?

A. X X O O O

B. X X X O O

C. O O O O O

D. X X X X X

E. It is not possible to determine the values in `A` after the code segment executes without knowing what values are in `A` before the code segment executes.

15. Consider the following code segment:

```
x = !y;
y = !x;
x = !y;
```

Assume that x and y are initialized boolean variables. Which of the following statements is true?

A. The final value of y is the same as the initial value of y.

B. The final value of x is the same as the initial value of x.

C. The final value of x is the same as the initial value of y.

D. The final value of y is the same as the initial value of x.

E. It is not possible to say anything about the final values of x and y without knowing their initial values.

Questions 16 and 17 refer to the following code segment (line numbers are included for reference). Assume that method `readInt` reads and returns one integer value.

```
 1  int x, sum;
 2  x = -1;
 3  sum = 1;
 4  x = readInt();
 5  while (x >= 0) {
 6     if (x > 0) {
 7         sum += x;
 8     }
 9     x = readInt();
10  }
11  System.out.println(sum);
```

16. For the purposes of this question, two code segments are considered to be *equivalent* if, when they are run using the same input, they produce the same output. Which line could be removed from the code segment given above so that the resulting code segment is equivalent to the original one?

   A. Line 2
   B. Line 3
   C. Line 4
   D. Line 7
   E. Line 9

17. The code segment given above was intended to read values until a negative value was read and then to print the sum of the positive values read. However, the code does not work as intended. Which of the following best describes the error?

   A. Variable x is not initialized correctly.
   B. Variable sum is not initialized correctly.
   C. Variable x is used before being initialized.
   D. Variable sum is used before being initialized.
   E. The negative value intended to signal end of input is included in the sum.

Questions 18 and 19 rely on the following information:

A dairy farm has 100 cows, kept in 5 fields, with 20 cows per field. The farmer needs a data structure to record the amount of milk given by each cow in one day.

Two different data structures are being considered:

Structure 1: An array of doubles of length 100. Each array entry is the amount of milk given by one cow on one day. The first 20 entries will be used for the cows in field 1, the next 20 entries will be used for the cows in field 2, and so on.

Structure 2: Five arrays of doubles, each of length 20. Each array entry is the amount of milk given by one cow on one day. The first array will be used for the cows in field 1, the second array will be used for the cows in field 2, and so on.

18. The following operations are to be performed on the data structure:

   Operation 1: Compute, for each of the five fields, the total amount of milk produced by the cows in that field.

   Operation 2: Compute the total amount of milk produced by all of the cows.

   Which of the following statements about these operations is true?

   A. Both operations can be implemented using either of the two data structures.

   B. Operation 1 can be implemented using either of the two data structures, but operation 2 can only be implemented using structure 1.

   C. Operation 2 can be implemented using either of the two data structures, but operation 1 can only be implemented using structure 1.

   D. Operation 1 can be implemented using either of the two data structures, but operation 2 can only be implemented using structure 2.

   E. Operation 2 can be implemented using either of the two data structures, but operation 1 can only be implemented using structure 2.

19. Under which of the following conditions does data structure 1 require more space than data structure 2?

   A. When the total amount of milk produced is the same for all five fields

   B. When the total amount of milk produced is different for each of the five fields

   C. When the cows in the first field produce the most milk, then the cows in the second field, then the cows in the third field, and so on.

   D. When the cows in the fifth field produce the most milk, then the cows in the fourth field, then the cows in the third field, and so on.

   E. Data structure 1 never requires more space than data structure 2.

20. Assume that variables s1 and s2 are both of type `String`. Consider the following three code segments:

Segment I	Segment II	Segment III
s1 = "hello";	s1 = "hello";	s1 = "hello";
s2 = s1;	s2 = s1;	s2 = s1 + "!";
	s1 = "bye";	

After executing which of the three segments will the expression s1 == s2 evaluate to `true`?

A. I only

B. II only

C. III only

D. I and II only

E. I, II, and III

21. Consider the following code segment:

```
int[] A = new int[3];
int[] B;

for (int j=0; j<A.length; j++) A[j] = j;
B = A;
for (int j=0; j<A.length; j++) A[j]++;
for (int j=0; j<A.length; j++) {
    System.out.print(A[j] + " " + B[j] + " ");
}
System.out.println();
}
```

What is printed when this code segment executes?

A. 0 0 1 1 2 2

B. 1 0 2 1 3 2

C. 1 1 2 2 3 3

D. 0 1 1 2 2 3

E. Nothing is printed because the use of B[j] in the print statement causes an `ArrayIndexOutOfBoundsException`.

Questions 22–25 involve reasoning about the GridWorld Case Study.

22. A class `newCritter` is defined as a subclass of `Critter`. The only method defined in the `newCritter` class is the `selectMoveLocation` method, given below (the `contains` method of the `ArrayList` class returns `true` iff its `Object` parameter is in the list).

```
public Location selectMoveLocation(ArrayList<Location> locs) {
    Location choice = getLocation().getAdjacentLocation(Location.SOUTH);
    if (locs.contains(choice)) return choice;
    else return null;
}
```

Which of the following best describes how a `newCritter` moves when its `act` method is called?

A. It always stays where it is.

B. It always removes itself from the grid.

C. If the location to the south is occupied, it moves to that location; otherwise, it stays where it is.

D. If the location to the south is empty, it moves to that location; otherwise, it removes itself from its grid.

E. If the location to the south contains a flower, it moves to that location; otherwise, it stays where it is.

For questions 23 and 24, assume that variable `act` is an `Actor` that is in a grid. Consider the following code fragment.

```
Location loc = act.getLocation();
Grid gr = act.getGrid();
int dir = act.getDirection();
boolean result = gr.get(loc.getAdjacentLocation(dir)) != null;
```

23. In which of the following cases might executing this code cause a method's precondition to be violated?

A. `act` is in an unbounded grid facing an occupied location.

B. `act` is in a bounded grid facing an occupied location.

C. `act` is in the last row of a bounded grid facing south.

D. `act` is in the first row of a bounded grid facing south.

E. `act` is in a bounded or unbounded grid facing an unoccupied location.

24. Assume that executing the code causes no preconditions to be violated. Which of the following best describes the conditions under which the code sets `result` to `true`?

A. When `act` is facing an empty location.

B. When `act` is facing an occupied location.

C. When `act` is facing a valid location.

D. When `act` is facing an invalid location.

E. When `act` is facing a location that contains a Bug.

25. Assume that the `Actor` class includes two private fields:

> `private Grid<E> myGrid;` keeps track of the actor's grid
>
> `private Location myLoc;` keeps track of the actor's location in its grid

An incomplete version of the `Actor` method `putSelfInGrid` is given below.

```
public void putSelfInGrid(Grid<Actor> gr, Location loc) {
// Preconditions: (1) this actor is not in a grid
//                (2) loc is valid in gr
    myGrid = gr;
    myLoc = loc;
    <missing code>
}
```

Which of the following would be the best replacement for `<missing code>` in the `putSelfInGrid` method above?

A. `if (gr.get(loc) != null) removeSelfFromGrid();`
   `gr.put(loc, this);`

B. `gr.put(loc, this);`
   `gr.remove(loc);`

C. `gr.remove(loc);`
   `moveTo(loc);`

D. `removeSelfFromGrid();`
   `gr.put(loc, this);`

E. `gr.put(loc, this);`
   `moveTo(loc);`

Questions 26 and 27 refer to the following Horse, WorkHorse, and RaceHorse classes (note that WorkHorse and RaceHorse are subclasses of Horse).

```java
public class Horse {
    private int age;
    private double price;

    // constructor
    public Horse(int a, double p) {
        age = a;
        price = p;
    }

    public int getAge() { return age; }

    public double getPrice() { return price; }

    public void setAge(int newAge) { age = newAge; }

    public void setPrice(double newPrice) { price = newPrice; }

    public void haveBirthday() {
        age++;
        price = price - .1*price;
    }
}

public class WorkHorse extends Horse {
    private double weight;

    // constructor
    public WorkHorse(int a, double p, double w) {
        super(a, p);
        weight = w;
    }
}

public class RaceHorse extends Horse {
    // constructor
    public RaceHorse(int a, double p) {
        super(a, p);
    }

    public void haveBirthday() {
        setAge( getAge()+1 );
        setPrice( getPrice() - .2*getPrice() );
    }
}
```

26. Which of the following statements will compile without error?

   A. `Horse h = new WorkHorse(2, 1000);`

   B. `Horse h = new RaceHorse(2, 1000);`

   C. `WorkHorse h = new RaceHorse(2, 1000);`

   D. `RaceHorse h = new WorkHorse(2, 1000);`

   E. `RaceHorse h = new Horse(2, 1000);`

27. Assume that variable h has been declared to be of type Horse, and has been initialized to represent a horse whose price is 100.
Which of the following statements about the call `h.haveBirthday()` is true?

   A. Whatever kind of horse variable h actually points to, the price of that horse after the call will be 90.

   B. Whatever kind of horse variable h actually points to, the price of that horse after the call will be 80.

   C. If variable h actually points to a RaceHorse object, then the price of that horse after the call will be 80.

   D. If variable h actually points to a WorkHorse object, there will be a runtime error, since class WorkHorse has no haveBirthday method.

   E. If variable h actually points to a WorkHorse object, the price of that horse after the call will still be 100, since class WorkHorse has no haveBirthday method.

28. Assume that variable A is a *sorted* array of ints. Consider the following code segment:

```
boolean flag = false;
for (int k=1; k<A.length; k++) {
    if (A[k-1] == A[k]) flag = true;
}
```

Which of the following best describes when variable flag is true after this code segment executes?

   A. Always

   B. Never

   C. If and only if array A contains duplicate values

   D. If and only if the last two values in array A are the same

   E. If and only if all values in array A are the same

Questions 29 and 30 refer to the following Shape class:

```
public class Shape {
   private int numSides;
   private String color;

   // constructor
   public Shape(int n) {
      numSides = n;
      color = "Black";
   }

   public void setColor(String newColor) {
      color = newColor;
   }

   public String getColor() {
      return color;
   }
}
```

29. Consider the following code segment, with line numbers included for reference:

```
1  Shape[] myShapes;
2  myShapes = new Shape[3];
3  myShapes[0].setColor("Red");
4  myShapes[0].setColor(myShapes[0].getColor() + "Blue");
5  myShapes[0].setColor(myShapes[0].getColor() + "Green");
6  System.out.print(myShapes[0].getColor());
```

What happens when this code executes?

A. Line 2 causes an `IndexOutOfBoundsException` because `myShapes` has length 0, and it cannot be changed to have length three.

B. Line 3 causes a `NullPointerException` because `myShapes[0]` has not been initialized.

C. There is no exception; `RedBlueGreen` is printed.

D. There is no exception; `BlackRedBlueGreen` is printed.

E. There is no exception; `GreenBlueRedBlack` is printed.

30. Consider the following instance variable and (incorrect) method:

```
private Shape[] myShapes;

public boolean sameColor(int k) {
// precondition: 0 <= k <  myShapes.length
//                myShapes contains no nulls
// postcondition: returns true iff some other shape in myShapes
//                has the same color as the shape at position k
    String col = myShapes[k].getColor();
    for (int j=0; j<myShapes.length; j++) {
       if (myShapes[j].getColor().equals(col)) return true;
    }
    return false;
}
```

As specified by its pre- and postconditions, method sameColor was intended to return true iff some other shape in the myShapes array has the same color as the shape at position k. However, when the method is tested, it is discovered that it *always* returns true. Which of the following changes would fix sameColor?

A. Change the condition of the *if* statement to
j!=k && myShapes[j].getColor().equals(col)

B. Change the condition of the *if* statement to
myShapes[j].getColor() == col

C. Change the condition of the *if* statement to
!myShapes[j].getColor().equals(col)

D. Replace the *if* statement with
return (myShapes[j].getColor().equals(col));

E. Replace the *if* statement with
return (myShapes[j].getColor() == col);

31. Consider the following two ways to determine whether the values in array A are in sorted order (from smallest to largest). Assume that A contains N values.

> **Idea 1:** For each index k between 0 and $N - 1$, check whether all elements with indexes larger than k have values greater than or equal to the value in A[k]; if so, the array is sorted.

> **Idea 2:** For each index k between 0 and $N - 2$, check whether the value in A[k+1] is greater than or equal to the value in A[k]; if so, the array is sorted.

Which of the following statements about the two ideas is true?

A. Only idea 1 will work.

B. Only idea 2 will work.

C. Both ideas will work; the two ideas will be equally efficient.

D. Both ideas will work; idea 1 will be more efficient than idea 2.

E. Both ideas will work; idea 2 will be more efficient than idea 1.

32. Method `isEven` below was intended to return `true` iff its parameter `num` is an even number; however, it does not always work as intended.

```
public static boolean isEven(int num) {
    if (num == 0) return true;
    else if (num > 0) return isEven(num-2);
    else return isEven(num+2);
}
```

Which of the following best describes what method `isEven` actually does?

A. Always returns `true`.

B. Returns `true` if `num` is a positive even number, and otherwise returns `false`.

C. Returns `true` if `num` is a negative even number, and otherwise returns `false`.

D. Returns `true` if `num` is an even number, and otherwise causes an infinite recursion.

E. Returns `true` if `num` is a positive even number, and otherwise causes an infinite recursion.

Questions 33 and 34 refer to the following recursive method:

```
public static int compute(int low, int high) {
    if ( low == high ) return 0;
    return 1 + compute(low+1, high);
}
```

33. When does a call `compute(low, high)` cause an infinite recursion?

A. Only when `low > high`.

B. Only when `high − low` is divisible by two.

C. Only when `high − low` is *not* divisible by two.

D. Only when `low < high`.

E. When `low != high`.

34. Which of the following best describes the value returned by a call `compute(low, high)` that does not cause an infinite recursion?

A. `low + high`

B. `low - high`

C. `high * low`

D. `high - low`

E. The sum of the numbers from `low` to `high`.

35. Consider the following instance variable and method:

```
private ArrayList<String> myList;

public String processList(int k) {
    if (k == myList.size()) return "";
    else return processList(k+1) + myList.get(k);
}
```

If `myList` is the list of strings shown below (with `"A"` in position 0 and `"D"` in position 3),

```
[ "A", "B", "C", "D" ]
```

what is returned by the call `processList(0)`?

A. `"ABC"`

B. `"ABCD"`

C. `"DCBA"`

D. `"AAAA"`

E. `"DDDD"`

36. Assume that classes `Person` and `Animal` have been defined, and that they each include a public `getName` method that returns a `String`. Also assume that a `Game` class includes the following instance variables and methods:

```
private Person[] personList;
private Animal[] animalList;

public boolean search(String personName) {
// search version 1: search for a person with the given name
   for (Person p : personList) {
      if (personName.equals(p.getName())) return true;
   }
   return false;
}

public boolean search(String animalName) {
// search version 2: search for an animal with the given name
   for (Animal an : animalList) {
      if (animalName.equals(an.getName())) return true;
   }
   return false;
}
```

Which of the following statements about this code is true?

A. It will not compile because the `Game` class includes two methods with the same names that have the same numbers and types of parameters.

B. It will not compile because the `Game` class includes an array of people and an array of animals.

C. It will compile. If a call to method `search` is made, the version that will execute will depend on whether `personList` or `animalList` is null.

D. It will compile. If a call to method `search` is made, the first version will be called first; if that version returns `false`, the second version will be called.

E. It will compile as long as every call to method `search` specifies which version should be called.

37. Consider the following instance variable and method:

```
private double[][] grid;

public boolean testGrid() {
    for (int j=0; j<grid[0].length; j++) {
        double val = grid[0][j];
        for (int k=1; k<grid.length; k++) {
            if (val > grid[k][j]) return false;
        }
    }
    return true;
}
```

Which of the following best describes the circumstances under which method `testGrid` returns `true`?

A. When for every column of the grid, the largest value for that column is in the last row

B. When for every column of the grid, the smallest value for that column is in the last row

C. When for every column of the grid, the largest value for that column is in the first row

D. When for every column of the grid, the smallest value for that column is in the first row

E. When for every column of the grid, all values for that column are the same

38. Consider the following code segment:

```
String s1 = "ab";
String s2 = s1;

s1 = s1 + "c";
System.out.println(s1 + " " + s2);
```

What is printed when this code executes?

A. abc ab

B. abc abc

C. ac ab

D. ac ac

E. ae ab

Questions 39 and 40 concern the following incomplete definition of class HorizontalLine.

```
public class HorizontalLine {
   private int startPoint;
   private int endPoint;

   // constructor
   // precondition: end > start
   public HorizontalLine(int start, int end) {
      startPoint = start;
      endPoint = end;
   }

   public int compareTo(Object other) {
   // Precondition: other is a HorizontalLine
   // Postcondition: returns -1 if this line is smaller than other;
   //                returns 0 if this line is the same as other;
   //                returns 1 if this line is greater than other
      HorizontalLine line = (HorizontalLine)other;
      : missing code
   }
}
```

A HorizontalLine object represents a horizontal line on the x-axis of a graph. For example:

HorizontalLine object's data fields   Corresponding line on the x-axis

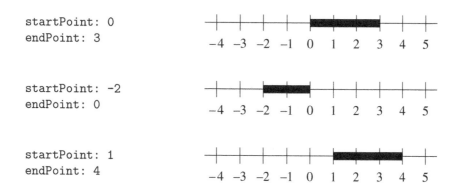

39. Which of the following could be used to replace *missing code* in the compareTo method so that lines are compared according to their *length* (i.e., line1 is considered to be less than line2 if line1 is shorter than line2; equal if their lengths are the same; and greater if line1 is longer than line2)?

A. `if (startPoint < line.startPoint && endPoint < line.endPoint) return -1;`
   `if (startPoint == line.startPoint && endPoint == line.endPoint) return 0;`
   `return 1;`

B. `if (startPoint < line.startPoint || endPoint < line.endPoint) return -1;`
   `if (startPoint == line.startPoint && endPoint == line.endPoint) return 0;`
   `return 1`

C. `if (startPoint < line.startPoint || endPoint < line.endPoint) return -1;`
   `if (startPoint == line.startPoint || endPoint == line.endPoint) return 0;`
   `return 1;`

D. `if (endPoint+startPoint < line.endPoint+line.startPoint) return -1;`
   `if (endPoint+startPoint == line.endPoint+line.startPoint) return 0;`
   `return 1;`

E. `if (endPoint-startPoint < line.endPoint-line.startPoint) return -1;`
   `if (endPoint-startPoint == line.endPoint-line.startPoint) return 0;`
   `return 1;`

40. Which of the following could be used to replace *missing code* in the compareTo method so that lines are compared according to their *starting position* (i.e., line1 is considered to be less than line2 if line1 starts to the left of line2; equal if they start at the same place; and greater if line1 starts to the right of line2)?

A. `if (startPoint < line.startPoint) return -1;`
   `if (startPoint == line.startPoint) return 0;`
   `return 1;`

B. `if (endPoint+startPoint < line.endPoint+line.startPoint) return -1;`
   `if (endPoint+startPoint == line.endPoint+line.startPoint) return 0;`
   `return 1;`

C. `if (startPoint < line.startPoint && endPoint < line.endPoint) return -1;`
   `if (startPoint == line.startPoint && endPoint == line.endPoint) return 0;`
   `return 1;`

D. `if (startPoint < line.startPoint || endPoint < line.endPoint) return -1;`
   `if (startPoint == line.startPoint && endPoint == line.endPoint) return 0;`
   `return 1;`

E. `if (startPoint < line.endPoint) return -1;`
   `if (startPoint == line.endPoint) return 0;`
   `return 1;`

Section II

Time: 1 hour and 45 minutes
Number of questions: 4
Percent of total grade: 50

Question 1

This question involves reasoning about the code from the GridWorld Case Study.

Assume that the `Grid` interface has been extended by adding two methods: `hasWind` and `getWindDirection`, defined below. The idea is that some locations in a grid will have wind blowing through them.

```
public boolean hasWind(Location loc)
// returns true iff location loc has wind blowing through it.
// Precondition: loc is valid in this grid

public int getWindDirection(Location loc)
// returns the direction in which the wind is blowing through location loc
// Precondition: loc is valid in this grid and has wind blowing through it
```

Now consider defining a new subclass of Bug called WindBug. A wind bug's actions are influenced by the wind blowing through the grid.

A wind bug can move iff all of the following conditions are met.

- The bug is in a grid.
- The location the bug is facing is valid.
- The location the bug is facing has no wind blowing through it, or the the wind is *not* blowing toward the bug's current location.

Part (a)

Complete the WindBug method isBlowingToward below. Method isBlowingToward should return true if there is wind blowing through location loc and that wind is blowing toward this wind bug's current location.

```
private boolean isBlowingToward(Location loc) {
// Return true iff there is wind blowing through location loc,
// and it is blowing toward this bug's current location.
//
// Precondition: (1) this bug is in a grid, and
//               (2) loc is valid in this bug's grid
```

Part (b)

Complete the WindBug method canMove below. In writing method canMove, you may call method isBlowingToward. Assume that isBlowingToward works as specified.

```
public boolean canMove() {
    // A wind bug can move iff all of the following conditions are met.
    //    1. The bug is in a grid.
    //    2. The location the bug is facing is valid.
    //    3. The location the bug is facing has no wind blowing through it,
    //       or the wind is not blowing toward the bug's current location.
```

Question 2

This question involves the following two (incomplete) class definitions, which define classes to be used for storing information about the students in an AP CS class.

```java
public class StudentInfo {
    private String name;
    private int[] grades;
    private double averageGrade;

    // constructor
    // precondition: theGrades is not null
    public StudentInfo( String theName, int[] theGrades ) {
        /* part (a) */
    }

    public String getName() { return name; }
    public double getAverageGrade() { return averageGrade; }
}

public class APCS {
    private StudentInfo[] students;
    private String highestAverage;

    // constructor
    public APCS() { /* part (b) */ }
}
```

Part (a)

Write the constructor for the StudentInfo class. The constructor should initialize the name and grades fields using the given values, and then it should compute the average grade and use that value to initialize the averageGrade field. (If the number of grades is zero, the averageGrade field should be set to zero.)

Complete the constructor below.

```java
// precondition: theGrades is not null
public StudentInfo( String theName, int[] theGrades ) {
```

Part (b)

Assume that the following methods can be used to read input values from a file:

```
public static int readInt()        // reads and returns the next
                                   // integer value
public static String readString()  // reads and returns the next
                                   // string value
```

Write the constructor for the APCS class. Assume that when the constructor is called, there is an input file ready for reading. The first piece of data in the file is a positive integer N, the number of students in the class. Then there is information for each of the N students, organized as follows:

- The student's name
- The number of grades recorded for that student
- The actual grades (integers in the range 0 to 100)

The APCS constructor should initialize its students field by creating an array of StudentInfo, using the data in the input file. It should then determine which student has the highest average and use that student's name to initialize its highestAverage field. (If two students share the same highest average, either name can be used to initialize the highestAverage field.)

For example, if the input data are as follows:

```
2
Jones
5
100 95 80 100 100
Smith
2
86 87
```

the students field should be initialized to contain two StudentInfo elements (one for Jones and one for Smith), and the highestAverage field should be initialized to "Jones", because Jones has an average grade of 95.0, whereas Smith has a (lower) average grade of 86.5.

In writing the APCS constructor, you may include calls to the StudentInfo constructor. Assume that the StudentInfo constructor works as specified.

Complete the APCS constructor below.

```
public APCS() {
```

Question 3

Part (a)

Write method findZero, as started below. Method findZero should return the index of the first element of array A that contains the value zero, starting from position pos. If no element of A from position pos to the end of the array contains the value zero, then findZero should return −1.

For example:

Array A	Position pos	Value returned by findZero(A, pos)
1 0 2 5 6	0	1
1 0 2 5 6	1	1
1 0 2 5 6	2	−1
1 0 2 0 6	0	1
1 0 2 0 6	1	1
1 0 2 0 6	2	3
1 2 3 4 5	0	−1

Complete method findZero below.

```
// precondition: 0 <= pos < A.length
// postcondition: returns the smallest index k such that
//                (pos <= k < A.length) and (A[k] == 0),
//                or -1 if there is no such index
public static int findZero(int[] A, int pos) {
```

Part (b)

Write method setZeros, as started below. Method setZeros should find the positions of the first two zeros in its array parameter A, and it should set all of the intervening values (if any) to zero. If A only contains one zero, if it contains no zeros, or if the first two zeros are right next to each other, setZeros should not modify A.

For example:

Array A before calling setZeros	Array A after the call setZeros(A)
0 1 2 0 4 0	0 0 0 0 4 0
1 0 2 3 4 0	1 0 0 0 0 0
1 2 0 0 4 5	1 2 0 0 4 5
1 0 2 3	1 0 2 3
1 2 3 4	1 2 3 4

In writing method setZeros, you may include calls to method findZero. Assume that method findZero works as specified.

Complete method setZeros below.

```
public static void setZeros( int[] A ) {
```

Question 4

For many board games (e.g., chess, checkers, and go), the board can be represented using a two-dimensional array of integers, where the value in position [j][k] tells which piece (if any) is currently at that position. When deciding what move to make next, it is often useful to look for certain important patterns on the board.

These ideas lead to the following (partially specified) classes:

```
public class Position {
   private int row;
   private int column;

   // constructor
   public Position(int theRow, int theCol) {
      row = theRow;
      col = theCol;
   }
}

public class BoardGame {
   private int[][] board;

   public BoardGame() { ... }  // constructor
   public Position patternPos( int[][] pattern ) { /* part (a) */ }
   public Position rotatedPatternPos(int[][] pattern ) { /* part (c) */ }

   /*** private method ***/
   private static int[][] rotate( int[][] A ) { /* part (b) */ }
}
```

Part (a)

Write the `patternPos` method of the `BoardGame` class. The `patternPos` method looks for the given pattern in the board array, and it returns the position in the board array where the upper-left corner of the pattern was found (if the pattern occurs more than once in the board array, the position corresponding to any of those occurrences can be returned). If the pattern does not occur in the board array, method `patternPos` returns `null`.

For example, assume that the board array is as follows:

1	2	3	4
5	6	7	8
9	10	11	12

Below are the results of some calls to `patternPos`.

pattern **Array**	**Value Returned by the Call** `patternPos( pattern )`
	(0,0)
	(1,1)
	(2,3)
	null
	null

<table>
<tr><td>1</td><td>2</td><td>3</td></tr>
<tr><td>5</td><td>6</td><td>7</td></tr>
</table>
(0,0)

<table>
<tr><td>6</td><td>7</td></tr>
<tr><td>10</td><td>11</td></tr>
</table>
(1,1)

<table>
<tr><td>12</td></tr>
</table>
(2,3)

<table>
<tr><td>6</td><td>2</td></tr>
<tr><td>7</td><td>3</td></tr>
</table>
null

<table>
<tr><td>1</td><td>3</td></tr>
<tr><td>5</td><td>7</td></tr>
</table>
null

Complete method `patternPos` below.

```
// precondition: both board and pattern are nonempty, rectangular
//               arrays
// postcondition: if pattern occurs in the board array, returns
//               the position in the array where the upper-
//               left-hand corner of the pattern was found;
//               otherwise, returns null
public Position patternPos( int[][] pattern ) {
```

Part (b)

Write the private `rotate` method of the `BoardGame` class. The `rotate` method should return a rectangular, two-dimensional array that contains the same values as its parameter A, but rotated 90 degrees clockwise. (The `BoardGame`'s `rotate` method can be used to rotate a given pattern so that it can be found in different orientations on the board.)

Below are some examples of calls to `rotate`.

Array A	Value Returned by the Call `rotate( A )`

Array A:

1	2	3
6	7	8

Value Returned:

6	1
7	2
8	3

Array A:

1	2	3	4	5
6	7	8	9	10

Value Returned:

6	1
7	2
8	3
9	4
10	5

Array A:

1	2	3	4	5
6	7	8	9	10
11	12	13	14	15

Value Returned:

11	6	1
12	7	2
13	8	3
14	9	4
15	10	5

Note that when array A is rotated, row 0 becomes the last column; row 1 becomes the second-to-last column, and so on.

Complete method `rotate` below.

```
// precondition: A is a nonempty, rectangular array
private static int[][] rotate( int[][] A ) {
```

Part (c)

Write the `rotatedPatternPos` method of the `BoardGame` class. The `rotatedPatternPos` method should look in the `board` array for the given pattern rotated 90, 180, or 270 degrees clockwise. It should return the position in the `board` array where the upper-left corner of the rotated pattern was found. If the rotated pattern occurs more than once in the `board` array, the position corresponding to any of those occurrences can be returned. If the rotated pattern does not occur in the `board` array, method `rotatedPatternPos` should return `null`.

For example, assume that the `board` array is as follows:

1	2	3	4
5	6	7	8
9	10	11	12

Below are the results of some calls to `rotatedPatternPos`.

pattern Array	Value Returned by the Call rotatedPatternPos(pattern)	Degrees of Rotation
3 7 / 2 6	(0,1)	90
7 6 / 3 2	(0,1)	180
6 2 / 7 3	(0,1)	270
4 8 12 / 3 7 11	(0,2)	90

In writing `rotatedPatternPos`, you may include calls to methods `patternPos` and `rotate`. Assume that those methods work as specified.

Complete method `rotatedPatternPos` below.

```
// precondition: both board and pattern are nonempty, rectangular
//               arrays
// postcondition: if pattern occurs in the board array rotated 90,
//                180, or 270 degrees clockwise, then returns the
//                position in the array where the upper-left-hand
//                corner of the pattern was found;
//                otherwise, returns null
public Position rotatedPatternPos( int[][] pattern ) {
```

Answers to Section I

1.	A	21.	C
2.	C	22.	D
3.	B	23.	C
4.	C	24.	B
5.	C	25.	E
6.	B	26.	B
7.	D	27.	C
8.	A	28.	C
9.	E	29.	B
10.	B	30.	A
11.	E	31.	E
12.	D	32.	D
13.	E	33.	A
14.	A	34.	D
15.	A	35.	C
16.	A	36.	A
17.	B	37.	D
18.	A	38.	A
19.	E	39.	E
20.	A	40.	A

Answers to Section II

Question 1
Part (a)

```
private boolean isBlowingToward(Location loc) {
  // Return true iff there is wind blowing through location loc,
  // and it is blowing toward this bug's current location.
  //
  // Precondition: (1) this bug is in a grid, and
  //               (2) loc is valid in this bug's grid.

    Grid gr = getGrid();
    if (!gr.hasWind(loc)) {
        return false;
    } else {
        int windDir = gr.getWindDirection(loc);
        int badDir = loc.getDirectionToward(getLocation());
        return (windDir == badDir);
    }
}
```

Part (b)

```
public boolean canMove() {
  // A wind bug can move iff all of the following conditions are met.
  //   1. The bug is in a grid.
  //   2. The location the bug is facing is valid.
  //   3. The location the bug is facing has no wind blowing through it,
  //      or the the wind is not blowing toward the bug's current location.
    // condition 1
        Grid<Actor> gr = getGrid();
        if (gr == null) return false;
    // condition 2
        Location loc = getLocation();
        int dir = getDirection();
        Location next = loc.getAdjacentLocation(dir);
        if (! gr.isValid(next)) return false;
    // condition 3
        return !isBlowingToward(next);
}
```

Grading Guide

Part (a) isBlowingToward   5 Points

+1   Check for wind in the location loc

+3   Check for wind blowing toward bug's current location

    +1   get wind direction in location loc

    +1   get direction from location loc to bug's current location

    +1   compare wind direction and direction to current location

+1   Return correct value

Part (b) canMove   4 Points

+1   Check for bug in a grid

    +1/2   get bug's grid

    +1/2   check if null

+2   Check for bug facing a valid location

    +11/2 get location toward which bug is facing

    +1/2   check if valid

+1/2 Correctly call isBlowingToward

+1/2 Return correct value

Question 2
Part (a)

```java
public StudentInfo( String theName, int[] theGrades ) {
    int sum = 0;

    name = theName;
    grades = theGrades;
    for (int oneGrade : grades) {
        sum += oneGrade;
    }
    if (grades.length > 0) {
        averageGrade = ((double)sum)/grades.length;
    }
    else averageGrade = 0;
}
```

Part (b)

```java
public APCS() {

    // initialize students array
    int numStudents = readInt();
    students = new StudentInfo[numStudents];
    for (int k=0; k<numStudents; k++) {
        String name = readString();
        int numGrades = readInt();
        int[] grades = new int[numGrades];
        for (int j=0; j<numGrades; j++) {
            grades[j] = readInt();
        }
        students[k] = new StudentInfo(name, grades);
    }

    // initialize highestAverage field
    double max = students[0].getAverageGrade();
    highestAverage = students[0].getName();
    for (int k=1; k<numStudents; k++) {
        double oneAv = students[k].getAverageGrade();
        if (oneAv > max) highestAverage = students[k].getName();
    }
}
```

Grading Guide

Part (a) The StudentInfo constructor   3 Points

+ 1/2   Initialization of name, grades

+2   Calculating the average grade

     + 1/2   loop attempt

     + 1/2   loop correct

     + 1/2   accumulate

     + 1/2   divide by length, including cast to double

+ 1/2   Set average grade to 0 if no grades

Part (b) The APCS constructor   6 Points

+1   Initialize array

     + 1/2   readInt

     + 1/2   array size

+1   Loop over numStudents

     + 1/2   attempt (must use value read in)

     + 1/2   correct

+ 1/2   Read values (name, number of grades, grades)

+1   Loop over grades

     + 1/2   loop

     + 1/2   readInt

+ 1/2   Initialize new StudentInfo

+2   Initialize highest average

     + 1/2   initialize

     + 1/2   loop

     + 1/2   comparison

     + 1/2   assign highest average

Question 3

Part (a)

Version 1: Use a *for-loop*, exiting the loop using a `return` statement as soon as possible.

```
public static int findZero(int[] A, int pos) {
   for (int k=pos; k<A.length; k++) {
      if (A[k] == 0) return k;
   }
   return -1;
}
```

Version 2: Use a *while-loop* whose condition checks both for having reached the end of the array and having found a zero.

```
public static int findZero(int[] A, int pos) {
   int k=pos;
   while (k<A.length && A[k]!=0) k++;
   if (k < A.length) return k;
   else return -1;
}
```

Note that the order of the expressions in the *while-loop* condition is very important; if it were written like this:

```
(A[k]!=0 && k<A.length)
```

there would be an out-of-bounds array access whenever there was no zero to be found in array A.

Part (b)

```
public static void setZeros(int[] A) {
   int first, second;

   // find the first zero in A
   first = findZero(A, 0);

   // if no zeros or only one zero, quit; otherwise find next zero
   if (first == -1 || first == A.length) return;
   second = findZero(A, first+1);

   // set all elements in the range first+1 - second-1 to zero
   for (int k=first+1; k<second; k++) {
      A[k] = 0;
   }
}
```

Grading Guide

Part (a) findZero   4 Points

+2   Loop over items in the array

    + 1/2   attempt

    + 1/2   correct starting value for search

    +1   correct loop

+1   Compare the current location to 0

+1   Return appropriate values

    + 1/2   return the index

    + 1/2   return -1

Part (b) setZeros   5 Points

+1   Find the first 0

    + 1/2   attempt (could include a reimplementation of part (a))

    + 1/2   correct (no reimplementation—must call findZero)

+1   Check for no zeroes or only one zero in array

+1   Find the second 0

+1   Loop through indices between the first and second 0

    + 1/2   attempt

    + 1/2   correct

+1   Assign all values within range to 0

Question 4

Part (a)

Note that method `patternPos` is much easier to write if you first write an auxiliary method that tests one position of the array to see whether there is a match using that position as the upper-left corner.

```
private boolean patternPosAux( int[][] pattern, int row, int col ) {
// precondition: pattern is a rectangular array;
//                 row < pattern.length;
//                 col < pattern[0].length
//                 row + pattern.length-1 < board.length
// postcondition: returns true if pattern occurs in board with its
//                 upper-left corner at board[row][col];
//                 otherwise, returns false
    int patRow = 0, patCol;
    int boardRow = row, boardCol = col;
    while (patRow < pattern.length && boardRow < board.length) {
        patCol = 0;
        boardCol = col;
        while (patCol < pattern[0].length && boardCol < board[0].length) {
            if (board[boardRow][boardCol] != pattern[patRow][patCol]) {
                return false;
            }
            patCol++;
            boardCol++;
        }
        patRow++;
        boardRow++;
    }
    return true;
}


public Position patternPos( int[][] pattern ) {
    for (int j=0; j<=board.length-pattern.length; j++) {
        for (int k=0; k<=board[0].length-pattern[0].length; k++) {
            if (patternPosAux(pattern, j, k)) {
                return new Position(j, k);
            }
        }
    }
    return null;
}
```

Part (b)

```
private static int[][] rotate( int[][] A ) {
   int[][] newA = new int[A[0].length][A.length];
   int newrow, newcol = A.length-1;
   for (int j=0; j<A.length; j++) {
      newrow = 0;
      for (int k=0; k<A[0].length; k++) {
         newA[newrow][newcol] = A[j][k];
         newrow++;
      }
      newcol--;
   }
   return newA;
}
```

Part (c)

Version 1: Use a loop to try each rotation in turn.

```
public Position rotatedPatternPos( int[][] pattern ) {
   int[][] tmp = rotate(pattern);
   int rotation = 90;
   while (rotation <= 270) {
      Position p = patternPos(tmp);
      if (p != null) return p;
      rotation +=90;
      tmp = rotate(tmp);
   }
   return null;
}
```

Version 2: Try each rotation explicitly.

```
public Position rotatedPatternPos1( int[][] pattern ) {
   int[][] tmp = rotate(pattern);
   Position p = patternPos(tmp);
   if (p != null) return p;
   tmp = rotate(tmp);
   p = patternPos(tmp);
   if (p != null) return p;
   tmp = rotate(tmp);
   p = patternPos(tmp);
   if (p != null) return p;
   return null;
}
```

Grading Guide

Part (a) `PatternPos`   4 Points

+ 1   Test all positions in board array as possible upper-left corner of pattern

+ 2   Test for pattern

      + 1   attempt

      + 1   correct

+ 1/2   Return position if pattern is found

+ 1/2   Return null otherwise

Part (b) `rotate`   3 Points

+ 1   Create new array of appropriate size

      + 1/2   declare array

      + 1/2   instantiate to correct size

+1 1/2   Traverse A copying to new array

      + 1/2   attempt row/col traversal

      + 1/2   copy some value from array based on traversal

      + 1/2   correct

+ 1/2   Return new array

Part (c) `rotatedPatternPos`   2 Points

+ 1   Check each rotation

      + 1/2   attempt

      + 1/2   correct

+ 1   Return appropriate values for each

Practice Examination A-4

Section I

Time: 1 hour and 15 minutes
Number of questions: 40
Percent of total grade: 50

1. Assume that x and y are variables of type `int`. Which of the following correctly tests whether the sum of x and y would be larger than the largest value that an `int` can have?

   A. `(Integer.MAX_VALUE - x) < y`
   B. `(Integer.MAX_VALUE - x) > y`
   C. `(x + y) > Integer.MAX_VALUE`
   D. `(x + y) >= Integer.MAX_VALUE`
   E. `(x + y) == (y + x)`

2. Consider the following code segment:

   ```
   x = (x || y);
   y = (x && y);
   ```

   Assume that x and y are initialized boolean variables. Which of the following statements is true?

   A. The final value of x is the same as the initial value of x.
   B. The final value of x is the same as the initial value of y.
   C. The final value of y is the same as the initial value of y.
   D. The final value of y is the same as the initial value of x.
   E. It is not possible to say anything about the final values of x and y without knowing their initial values.

3. Assume that `A` is an `ArrayList` and that `val` is a non-null `Object`. Consider the following code segment:

```
boolean tmp = false;
for (Object ob : A) {
    if (!tmp) tmp = (val.equals(ob));
}
return tmp;
```

Which of the following best characterizes the conditions under which this code segment returns true?

A. Whenever `A` contains value `val`

B. Whenever the first item in `A` has value `val`

C. Whenever the last item in `A` has value `val`

D. Whenever more than one item in `A` has value `val`

E. Whenever exactly one item in `A` has value `val`

4. Consider the following instance variable and method:

```
private String word;

public boolean findWord( String bigWord ) {
    int index = bigWord.indexOf( word );
    return ( (index > 0) &&
             (index + word.length() < bigWord.length()) );
}
```

For which of the following values of `bigWord` and `word` will method `findWord` return true?

	bigWord	word
A.	hello	he
B.	pallid	aid
C.	apple	ape
D.	nicety	ice
E.	solid	lid

5. Assume that two classes, `Plant` and `Animal`, and two interfaces, `Tropical` and `Spotted`, have been defined. Consider defining a new class named `Mold`. Which of the following statements is true?

   A. The `Mold` class can extend at most one of the `Plant` and `Animal` classes, and it can implement at most one of the `Tropical` and `Spotted` interfaces.

   B. The `Mold` class can extend at most one of the `Plant` and `Animal` classes, but it can implement both the `Tropical` and `Spotted` interfaces.

   C. The `Mold` class can extend both the `Plant` and `Animal` classes, but it can implement at most one of the `Tropical` and `Spotted` interfaces.

   D. The `Mold` class can extend both the `Plant` and `Animal` classes, and it can implement both the `Tropical` and `Spotted` interfaces.

   E. If the `Mold` class implements both the `Tropical` and `Spotted` interfaces, it can extend at most one of the `Plant` and `Animal` classes. If it implements just one of the `Tropical` and `Spotted` interfaces, it can extend both the `Plant` and `Animal` classes.

6. Consider the following code segment:

   ```
   if (n > 0) n = -n;
   if (n < 0) n = 0;
   ```

   This segment is equivalent to which of the following?

   A. `n = 0;`
   B. `if (n > 0) n = 0;`
   C. `if (n < 0) n = 0;`
   D. `if (n > 0) n = -n; else n = 0;`
   E. `if (n < 0) n = 0; else n = -n;`

7. Consider the following two code segments:

Segment 1	Segment 2

```
Segment 1

while (k > 0) {
    System.out.println(k);
    k--;
}
```

```
Segment 2

while (k > 0) {
    System.out.println(k);
    k--;
}
while (k > 0) {
    System.out.println(k);
    k--;
}
```

Assume that in both cases variable k has the *same* initial value. Under which of the following conditions will the two code segments produce identical output?

I. The initial value of k is greater than zero.
II. The initial value of k is zero.
III. The initial value of k is less than zero.

A. I only

B. II only

C. III only

D. I and III only

E. I, II, and III

8. In Java, the && operator has higher precedence than the || operator. Suppose you didn't know that, and you wanted to write some code that would let you find out. Which of the following expressions could you use; that is, which expression evaluates to two different values depending on the relative precedences of the two operators?

A. true || false && true

B. true || true && false

C. false || false && true

D. false || true && true

E. false || true && false

9. Consider designing a data structure to store a "to-do" list: a list of tasks (strings). For example, a to-do list might include the following:

    shop
    take bath
    eat lunch
    walk dog
    clean garage

    Assume that the operations to be performed on a to-do list include the following:

    - add a new task to the list
    - remove and return one task from the list

    and that an `ArrayList<String>` is used to store the to-do list. Which of the following is the most efficient way to implement the add and remove operations?

    A. Add and remove tasks at the beginning of the list.
    B. Add and remove tasks at the end of the list.
    C. Add tasks at the beginning of the list, and remove them from the end of the list.
    D. Add tasks at the end of the list, and remove them from the beginning of the list.
    E. Add tasks at the beginning of the list, and remove them from randomly selected positions in the list.

10. Consider the following incomplete code segment:

```
int sum=0;
for ( int k=0; condition; k++ ) {
    statement1;
}
statement2;
```

    Assume that variable `A` is an array of `int`s. Which of the following can be used to replace the placeholders *condition*, *statement1*, and *statement2* so that the code segment computes and returns the sum of the values in `A`?

	condition	statement1	statement2
A.	`k < A.length`	`sum++`	`System.out.println(sum)`
B.	`k < A.length`	`sum += A[k]`	`return sum`
C.	`k <= A.length`	`sum += A[k]`	`return sum`
D.	`k <= A.length`	`sum++`	`return sum`
E.	`k <= A.length`	`sum += A[k]`	`System.out.println(sum)`

11. Which of the following statements about the relative efficiencies of Insertion Sort and Merge Sort is/are true?

    I. Merge Sort is faster when the values are initially in sorted order.
    II. Insertion Sort is faster when the values are initially in sorted order.
    III. Merge Sort is faster when the values are initially in *reverse* sorted order.

    A. I only

    B. II only

    C. III only

    D. I and III

    E. II and III

12. A program is being written by a team of programmers. One programmer is implementing a class called `Employee`; another programmer is writing code that will use the `Employee` class. Which of the following aspects of the public methods of the `Employee` class does *not* need to be known by both programmers?

    A. The methods' names

    B. The methods' return types

    C. What the methods do

    D. How the methods are implemented

    E. The numbers and types of the methods' parameters

13. Suppose that you want to know whether an array of integer values, stored in *unsorted order*, contains the value zero. Which of the following is the best way to find out?

    A. Use sequential search.

    B. Use binary search.

    C. Sort the array using Merge Sort, then use sequential search.

    D. Sort the array using Merge Sort, then use binary search.

    E. Compute the product of the values in the array and see if the result is zero.

14. Which of the following best explains what is meant by *overloading* a method?

    A. Defining another method that does the same thing

    B. Defining another method with the same number of parameters

    C. Defining another method with the same parameter names

    D. Defining another method with the same precondition

    E. Defining another method with the same name but different numbers or types of parameters

Questions 15 and 16 concern the following two class definitions:

```java
public class Liquid {
   private int amount;

   // constructor
   public Liquid() {
      System.out.print("liquid ");
      amount = 0;
   }

   public int getAmount() { return amount; }
   public void setAmount(int am) { amount = am; }
}

public class Milk extends Liquid {
   private int percentFat;

   // constructor
   public Milk(int percent) {
      System.out.print("milk ");
      percentFat = percent;
   }
}
```

15. Consider the following code segment:

```java
Liquid liq = new Milk(2);
Milk mil = new Milk(4);
```

What is printed when this code executes?

A. `milk milk`

B. `liquid milk`

C. `liquid liquid`

D. `liquid milk liquid milk`

E. `milk liquid milk liquid`

16. Consider the following code segment:

```
Liquid water = new Liquid();
Liquid rain = water;
rain.setAmount(10);
water.setAmount(20);
water = new Liquid();
System.out.println(water.getAmount() + " " + rain.getAmount());
```

What is printed when this code executes?

A. 0 0

B. 0 10

C. 0 20

D. 20 10

E. 20 20

17. Consider the following instance variable and method.

```
private int A[][];

public int doSomething() {
    int j = 0;
    int k = 0;
    int result = A[j][k];
    while (j<A.length) {
        if (A[j][k] < result) result = A[j][k];
        j++;
    }
    return result;
}
```

Which of the following best describes what method doSomething does?

A. Returns the smallest value in A.

B. Returns the smallest value in the first column of A.

C. Returns the smallest value in the first row of A.

D. Returns the index of the column that contains the smallest value in A.

E. Returns the index of the row that contains the smallest value in A.

18. Consider adding a new version of the add method to the `java.util.ArrayList<E>` class. The header for the new method is shown below.

```
public void add(E x, boolean toFront)
```

If parameter `toFront` is `true`, the new method adds x to the front of the list; otherwise, it adds x to the end of the list.

Which of the following statements about this proposal is true?

A. The new method can be added to the `ArrayList<E>` class.

B. The new method cannot be added to the `ArrayList<E>` class because that class already has a method that adds an item to the end of the list.

C. The new method cannot be added to the `ArrayList<E>` class because that class already has a method with the same name.

D. The new method cannot be added to the `ArrayList<E>` class because that class already has a method with the same name and with two parameters, one of which has type E.

E. The new method as defined above cannot be added to the `ArrayList<E>` class; however, if the parameters were specified in the opposite order, `public void add(boolean toFront, E x)`, the new method could be added to the `ArrayList<E>` class.

19. Consider the following instance variable and incomplete method:

```
private double[][] A;

public boolean isInRow( double val, int r ) {
// precondition: A is a rectangular array with at least r+1 rows
// postcondition: returns true iff val is in row r of A
    for (int col=0; col<A[0].length; col++) {
        statement1
    }
    statement2


}
```

Which of the following replacements for *statement1* and *statement2* could be used to complete the `isInRow` method so that it works as specified by its pre- and post-conditions?

	statement1	*statement2*
A.	`return (val == A[r][col]);`	`return true;`
B.	`return (val == A[r][col]);`	`return false;`
C.	`return (val != A[r][col]);`	`return true;`
D.	`if (val == A[r][col]) return true;`	`return false;`
E.	`if (val != A[r][col]) return false;`	`return true;`

Questions 20–22 involve reasoning about the GridWorld Case Study.

20. Which of the following `Actor` methods might cause a different `Actor` to be removed from a grid?

    I.   `putSelfInGrid`
    II. `removeSelfFromGrid`
    III. `act`

    A. I only
    B. II only
    C. III only
    D. I and II
    E. I and III

21. Which of the following conditions must be true for a Bug to be able to move?

    A. The Bug is facing north.
    B. The Bug is in a grid.
    C. The Bug has at least one unoccupied adjacent location.
    D. The adjacent location toward which the Bug is facing is empty.
    E. The Bug has at least one adjacent location that contains another Bug.

22. Consider the bounded grid shown below, where B means a Bug, C means a `Critter`, F means a `Flower`, and R means a `Rock`.

R	B
R	C
F	C

    If the `act` method of the `Critter` in location (1,1) is called, where might the `Critter` move?

    A. (0,0)
    B. (0,2)
    C. (1,0)
    D. (0,1)
    E. (2,1)

23. Consider the following instance variable and method:

```
private List<String> myList;

public boolean checkList() {
// precondition: myList.size() > 0 and myList contains no nulls
   for (int k=0; k<myList.size()-1; k++) {
      if (myList.get(k).compareTo(myList.get(k+1) < 0) return false;
   }
   return true;
}
```

Which of the following best characterizes the lists for which method `checkList` returns `true`?

A. Lists that contain duplicate values

B. Lists that are sorted in lexicographic order

C. Lists that are sorted in reverse lexicographic order

D. Lists that contain a string that represents a negative number

E. Lists that do not contain a string that represents a negative number

24. Consider the following recursive method:

```
public static void printArray(String[] A, int k) {
   if (k < A.length) {
      printArray(A, k+1);
      System.out.print(A[k]);
   }
}
```

Assume that array `A` has been initialized to be of length four and to contain the values `"a"`, `"b"`, `"c"`, and `"d"` (with `"a"` in `A[0]`, `"b"` in `A[1]`, and so on). What is output as a result of the call `printArray(A,0)`?

A. bcd

B. dcb

C. abcd

D. dcba

E. dddd

Questions 25 and 26 refer to the following method:

```
public static int count(String s1, String s2) {
    int num = 0;
    for (int k=0; k<s1.length(); k++) {
        if (s1.substring(k, k+1).equals(s2.substring(k, k+1))) num++;
    }
    return num;
}
```

25. What will be returned by the call count("abcde", "fecca")?

    A. 0

    B. 1

    C. 2

    D. 3

    E. 4

26. Which of the following calls will cause a StringIndexOutOfBoundsException?

    I.   count("", "");

    II. count("abc", "abcd");

    III. count("abcd", "abc");

    A. I only

    B. II only

    C. III only

    D. II and III

    E. I, II, and III

27. Which of the following operations can be implemented to work more efficiently on an ArrayList of Integers if the values in the list are in sorted order?

    A. Searching for a given value in the list

    B. Adding a new value to the list

    C. Removing the value in a given position in the list

    D. Printing all values in the list

    E. Computing the sum of all values in the list

28. Assume that A is a nonempty array of strings. Consider the following code segment:

```
int x = 0;
for (int k=1; k<A.length; k++) {
    if (A[k].compareTo(A[x]) < 0) x = k;
}
return A[x];
```

Which of the following best describes what this code segment does?

A. It returns the index of the string in A that comes before all other strings in A in lexicographic order.

B. It returns the index of the string in A that comes after all other strings in A in lexicographic order.

C. It returns the string in A that comes before all other strings in A in lexicographic order.

D. It returns the string in A that comes after all other strings in A in lexicographic order.

E. It is not possible to determine what the code segment does without knowing how A is initialized.

29. Consider the following recursive method (assume that method readInt reads the next integer value from a file):

```
public static void printVals(int n) {
    if (n > 0) {
        int x = readInt();
        printVals(n-1);
        if (x > 0) System.out.print(x + " ");
    }
}
```

Assume that the input file contains the values:

```
10  -10  20  -20  30  -30
```

What is printed as a result of the call printVals(3)?

A. 10 20

B. 20 10

C. 10 20 30

D. 10 -10 20

E. 20 -10 10

30. Assume that the following declarations have been made.

```
String s;
ArrayList A;
```

Note that A is declared to be a "plain" `ArrayList`, not an `ArrayList` of strings. Consider the following statement:

```
if (A.size() != 0) s = (String)A.get(0);
```

Which of the following statements about this statement is true?

A. The statement would compile and execute without error whether or not the cast is used.

B. The statement would compile without error whether or not the cast is used, but the use of the cast prevents a runtime error when the first item in A is not a `String`.

C. The statement would compile without error whether or not the cast is used, but there will be a runtime error if the first item in A is not a `String` whether or not the cast is used.

D. The statement would cause a compile-time error if the cast were not used, and the use of the cast also prevents a runtime error if the first item in A is not a `String`.

E. The statement would cause a compile-time error if the cast were not used, and there will be a runtime error if the first item in A is not a `String` even though the cast is used.

31. Consider designing classes to represent different kinds of animals: mammals, reptiles, birds, and insects. Which of the following is the best design?

A. Use five unrelated classes: `Animal`, `Mammal`, `Reptile`, `Bird`, and `Insect`.

B. Use one class, `Animal`, with four fields: `Mammal`, `Reptile`, `Bird`, and `Insect`.

C. Use one class, `Animal`, with four subclasses: `Mammal`, `Reptile`, `Bird`, and `Insect`.

D. Use five classes, `Animal`, `Mammal`, `Reptile`, `Bird`, and `Insect`, with `Mammal` as a subclass of `Animal`, `Reptile` as a subclass of `Mammal`, and so on.

E. Use four classes, `Mammal`, `Reptile`, `Bird`, and `Insect`, each with an `Animal` subclass.

Questions 32 and 33 refer to the following recursive method:

```
public static int compute(int x, int y) {
   if (x > y) return x;
   else return( compute(x+2, y-2) );
}
```

32. What is returned by the call compute(1, 5)?

   A. 1

   B. 3

   C. 5

   D. 7

   E. No value is returned because an infinite recursion occurs.

33. Which of the following best characterizes the circumstances under which the call compute(x, y) leads to an infinite recursion?

   A. Never

   B. Whenever x = y

   C. Whenever x < y

   D. Whenever x > y

   E. Whenever both x and y are odd

34. Assume that p and q are String variables and that the expression

   (p != q)

evaluates to true. Which of the following must also evaluate to true?

   I.   !p.equals(q)
   II. p.length() != q.length()
   III. (p!=null) || (q!=null)

   A. I only

   B. II only

   C. III only

   D. I and II

   E. I and III

35. Consider the following instance variable and methods. Assume that method `myListContains` is implemented correctly.

```
private ArrayList myList;

public ArrayList combine(ArrayList A) {
    ArrayList result = new ArrayList();

    // copy all items from myList into result
    for (Object ob : myList) {
        result.add(ob);
    }

    // now add items in list A that are not already in result
    for (Object ob : A) {
        if (! myListContains(ob)) result.add(ob);
    }
    return result;
}

private boolean myListContains(Object ob) {
    // returns true iff ob is in myList
        : code not shown
}
```

Method `combine` was intended to create and return a list containing all items that are in either `myList` or A. If an item occurs more than once in one or both of those lists, the number of those items in the returned list should be the *maximum* of the number in `myList` and the number in list A.

For which of the following pairs of lists does method `combine` fail to work correctly?

	myList	A
A.	[0, 1, 2]	[0, 1, 2, 2]
B.	[0, 1, 2, 2]	[0, 1, 2]
C.	[0, 1, 2, 2]	[0, 1]
D.	[0, 1, 2, 2]	[0, 1, 2, 2]
E.	[0, 1]	[0, 2]

36. Assume that `val` is an `int` variable initialized to be greater than zero and that `A` is an array of `ints`. Consider the following code segment:

```
for (int k=0; k<A.length; k++) {
    while (A[k] < val) {
        A[k] *= 2;
    }
}
```

Which of the following best describes when this code segment will go into an infinite loop?

A. Always

B. Whenever `A` includes a value greater than `val`

C. Whenever `A` includes a value less than `val`

D. Whenever `A` includes a value equal to `val`

E. Whenever `A` includes a value less than or equal to zero

37. Assume that a subclass of the `ArrayList<E>` class, called `NewList<E>`, has been defined, including the method specified below.

```
public void add(E x) {
    // postcondition: adds x to the front of the list
    :
}
```

Note that the `ArrayList<E>` class has an add method with the same signature. Consider the following code segment:

```
ArrayList<Integer> L1 = new ArrayList<Integer>();
ArrayList<Integer> L2 = new NewList<Integer>();
L1.add(new Integer(5));
L2.add(new Integer(5));
```

Which of the following statements about the two calls to add is true?

A. Both calls will call the add method of the `ArrayList<E>` class, because both L1 and L2 are empty when the calls are made.

B. Both calls will call the add method of the `ArrayList<E>` class, because both L1 and L2 are declared to be `ArrayList<E>`.

C. Both calls will call the add method of the `NewList<E>` class, because that method has overridden the add method of the `ArrayList<E>` class.

D. Both calls will call the add method of the `ArrayList<E>` class, because that is a standard java class, whereas `NewList<E>` is a user-defined class.

E. The first call will call the add method of the `ArrayList<E>` class because L1 holds a reference to an `ArrayList<E>`, and the second call will call the add method of the `NewList<E>` class because L2 holds a reference to a `NewList<E>`.

Questions 38 and 39 refer to the following incomplete definitions of the Book and Biography classes (note that Biography is a subclass of Book).

```
public class Book {
    private String title;
    private boolean fiction;

    // constructor
    public Book(String aTitle, boolean isFiction) {
        title = aTitle;
        fiction = isFiction;
    }

    // other methods not shown
}

public class Biography extends Book {
    private String name;

    // constructor
    public Biography(String aTitle, String aName) {
        : missing code
    }

    // other methods not shown
}
```

38. When a Biography object is created, its title and name fields should be initialized to the given values, and its fiction field should be initialized to false. Which of the following statements should be used to replace *missing code* to implement the Biography constructor correctly?

    A. `super(aTitle, aName, false);`

    B. `super(aTitle);`
       `name = aName;`
       `fiction = false;`

    C. `title = aTitle;`
       `name = aName;`
       `fiction = false;`

    D. `super(aTitle, false);`
       `name = aName;`

    E. `name = aName;`
       `super(aTitle, false);`

39. Suppose we want to keep track of the total number of Book objects ever created. Which of the following is the best way to do this?

A. Add a static field to the Book class, and increment that field in the Book constructor.

B. Add a non static field to the Book class, and set that field to 1 in the Book constructor.

C. Define a new class called numBooks, and create a numBooks object every time a Book object is created.

D. Add a non static field to the Book class, and add a third parameter to the Book constructor so that every call to the constructor can pass the correct value.

E. Define a new numBooks interface, and make the Book class implement that interface.

40. Assume that A and B are arrays of ints, both of the same length. Which of the following code segments returns true if and only if the two arrays contain the same sequence of values?

A. `return (A == B);`

B. `return (A.equals(B));`

C.
```
for (int k=0; k < A.length; k++) {
    if (A[k] != B[k]) return false;
}
return true;
```

D.
```
for (int k=0; k < A.length; k++) {
    if (A[k] == B[k]) return true;
}
return false;
```

E.
```
boolean match;
for (int k=0; k < A.length; k++) {
    match = (A[k] == B[k]);
}
return match;
```

Section II

Time: 1 hour and 45 minutes
Number of questions: 4
Percent of total grade: 50

Question 1

This question involves reasoning about the code from the GridWorld Case Study.

Consider a new subclass of Bug called TravelerBug. A traveler bug keeps track of the locations in its grid that it has visited. A traveler bug can move as long as there is a location in the grid that it has not yet visited, and that is occupied by an actor that is not a TravelerBug.

A partial declaration for the TravelerBug class is given below.

```
public class TravelerBug extends Bug {

    // list of the locations that this traveler bug has visited
    private List<Location> visitedList;

    public TravelerBug() {
    // constructor: initialize VisitedList to be empty
        visitedList = new ArrayList<Location>();
    }

    private ArrayList<Location> getMoveLocs() { /* part (a) */ }

    public void move(List<Location> moveLocs) { /* part (b) }

    public void act() { /* part (c) /* }

    private boolean isVisited( Location loc ) {
      // return true iff loc is in visitedList
      : actual code not shown
    }
}
```

Part (a)

Write method getMoveLocs, which should return a list of the occupied locations in the grid that do not contain a traveler bug, and that this traveler bug has not yet visited. If there are no such locations, getMoveLocs should return an empty list. You may include calls to isVisited without writing the code for that method.

Complete method getMoveLocs below.

```
private ArrayList<Location> getMoveLocs( ) {
    // Precondition: this traveler bug is in a grid
    // Return a list of the occupied locations that do not contain
    // a traveler bug, and that this traveler bug has not visited,
    // or an empty list if there are no such locations
```

Part (b)

Write method move, which should work as follows:

- Choose a random location in moveLocs and move there.
- After moving, add the chosen location to visitedList.

Complete method move below.

```
public void move(List<Location> moveLocs) {
// Precondition: moveLocs.size() > 0
```

Part (c)

Write method act, which should work as follows:

- Get a list of occupied locations in the grid that do not contain a traveler bug, and that this traveler bug has not yet visited.
- If the list is empty, remove this traveler bug from the grid.
- Otherwise, cause this traveler bug to move to one of the locations in the list, correctly updating its visitedList.

You may include calls to methods getMoveLocs and move. Assume that they work as specified.

Complete method act below.

```
public void act( ) {
// Precondition: this traveler bug is in a grid
```

Question 2

A laundry uses a Java program to keep track of its customers and their orders. One class, LaundryOrder, will be used to keep track of an individual order. Each LaundryOrder object will need to include the following information:

- The name of the customer
- The number of items to be cleaned
- Whether the order is ready

The LaundryOrder class must provide the following operations:

- Create a LaundryOrder object given a customer name and number of items.
- Access the customer name, the number of items, and whether the order is ready.
- Change the object to show that the order is ready.

Part (a)

Write a complete declaration for the LaundryOrder class.

Part (b)

The laundry also does alterations on items brought in for cleaning, and an AlterationOrder class will be used to keep track of alteration orders. An AlterationOrder is a LaundryOrder with the following additional properties:

- An AlterationOrder includes a string that specifies what is to be done (the alteration instructions).
- Alterations are performed on only one item, therefore the number of items is always 1.
- The alteration instructions can be accessed but not modified.

Write a complete declaration for the AlterationOrder class.

Part (c)

To keep track of all current orders, the laundry uses the Laundry class partially declared below.

```
public class Laundry {

    private ArrayList<LaundryOrder> allOrders;

    // constructor not shown

    // returns an ArrayList containing the LaundryOrders in allOrders
    // that are not ready
    public ArrayList<LaundryOrder> unfinishedOrders() { /* part (c) */ }

    // other methods not shown
}
```

The unfinishedOrders method returns an ArrayList containing all of the LaundryOrders in the allOrders ArrayList that are not yet ready.

Complete method unfinishedOrders below.

```
// returns an ArrayList containing the LaundryOrders in allOrders
// that are not ready
public ArrayList<LaundryOrder> unfinishedOrders() {
```

Question 3

This question involves the two classes partially defined below. The Person class is used to store information about one person; the Family class is used to store information about a family (containing zero or more people). The Family class contains a field called peopleList that is a list of the people in the family, sorted by age (from youngest to oldest).

```java
public class Person {
   private String name;
   private int age;
   private int numSameAge;  // number of other people in same family
                            // with same age as this person

   // constructor
   public Person(String theName, int theAge) {
      name = theName;
      age = theAge;
      numSameAge = 0;
   }
   public String getName() { return name; }
   public int getAge() { return age; }
   public int getNumSameAge() { return numSameAge; }
   public void setNumSameAge( int n ) { numSameAge = n; }
}


public class Family {
   private List<Person> peopleList; // list of people in this family,
                                    // sorted by age (from youngest
                                    // to oldest)

   // constructor
   public Family() {
      peopleList = new ArrayList<Person>();
   }

   // adds person p to this family
   public void addPerson(Person p) { /* part (b) */ }

   /*** private method ***/
   private int personBeforePos(int age) { /* part (a) */ }
}
```

Part (a)

Write the personBeforePos method of the Family class. Method personBeforePos should search through peopleList, looking for the person whose age is closest to the value of parameter age without being larger. It should return the position of that person in the list. If there is no such person (i.e., if the list is empty or all ages are greater than the value of parameter age), method personBeforePos should return -1. If there is more than one person with the same, closest age, method personBeforePos should return the position of the *last* such person in the list.

Complete method personBeforePos below.

```
// precondition: the peopleList field contains a list of Person
//               sorted by age (from youngest to oldest)
//
// postcondition:  returns the position in peopleList of the person
//                 in this family whose age is closest to the given
//                 age without being larger;
//                 returns -1 if there are no people in this family
//                 at all, or none whose age is less than or equal to
//                 the given age
private int personBeforePos(int age) {
```

Part (b)

Write the addPerson method of the Family class. Method addPerson should add person p to the family, so that the family's list of people is still sorted by age (from youngest to oldest). If there are any other people in the family with the same age as p, their numSameAge fields (and that of person p) should be set to the correct values.

In writing method addPerson, you may include calls to method personBeforePos. Assume that personBeforePos works as specified.

Complete method addPerson below.

```
// precondition: the peopleList field is sorted by age (from youngest
//               to oldest) and all numSameAge fields are correct
// postcondition: p has been added to peopleList in sorted order (by age)
//                and all numSameAge fields are correct
public void addPerson(Person p) {
```

Question 4

The `Orchard` class partially defined below is used to represent a kiwi orchard in which the kiwi vines are planted in a rectangular grid. Grid coordinates are represented using the `Position` class, also defined below.

```
public class Position {
    private int row;
    private int column;

    // constructor
    public Position(int initX, int initY) {
        row = initRow;
        column = initColumn;
    }

    public int getRow() { return x; }
    public int getColumn() { return y; }
}

public class Orchard {
    private String[][] plants; // each array element is either
                               // "male" or "female"

    public boolean willFruit( Position p ) { /* part (a) */ }
    public ArrayList<Position> willNotFruit() { /* part (b) */ }
}
```

Each kiwi plant is either male or female. The `plants` array (which is a private field of the `Orchard` class) keeps track of the genders of the plants in the orchard: Each element of the array contains a string, either `"male"` or `"female"`, depending on the gender of the plant in that position.

In order to produce fruit, a female plant must have a male plant no more than two positions away horizontally or vertically, or no more than one position away diagonally. For example, consider the orchard represented using the following array:

	0	1	2	3	4
0	male	female	female	female	female
1	female	female	female	female	male
2	female	**female**	**female**	female	female

In this orchard, the plants shown in bold (in positions (2,1) and (2,2)) will not produce fruit because no male plant is close enough to them.

Part (a)

Write the `Orchard` class's `willFruit` method. The method should return `true` if and only if the female plant at the given position will produce fruit.

Complete method `willFruit` below.

```
// precondition: Position p is inside the plants array and
//               the plant at position p is female
public boolean willFruit( Position p ) {
```

Part (b)

Write the `Orchard` class's `willNotFruit` method. The method should return an `ArrayList` containing the `Positions` of all of the female plants in the orchard that will not fruit. For example, for the orchard shown above, the method would return a list containing two `Positions`: (2,1) and (2,2).

In writing method `willNotFruit`, you may include calls to method `willFruit`. Assume that method `willFruit` works as specified.

Complete method `willNotFruit` below.

```
// postcondition: returns an ArrayList containing the Positions
//                of all of the female plants in the orchard
//                that will not fruit
public ArrayList<Position> willNotFruit() {
```

Answers to Section I

1.	A	21.	B
2.	C	22.	D
3.	A	23.	C
4.	D	24.	D
5.	B	25.	B
6.	A	26.	C
7.	E	27.	A
8.	B	28.	C
9.	B	29.	B
10.	B	30.	E
11.	E	31.	C
12.	D	32.	C
13.	A	33.	A
14.	E	34.	C
15.	D	35.	A
16.	C	36.	E
17.	B	37.	E
18.	A	38.	D
19.	D	39.	A
20.	E	40.	C

Answers to Section II

Question 1

Part (a)

```
public ArrayList<Location> getMoveLocs( ) {
// Precondition: this bug is in a grid
// Return a list of the occupied locations that do not contain
// a traveler bug, and that this traveler bug has not visited,
// or an empty list if there are no such locations

    Grid<Actor> myGrid = getGrid();
    ArrayList<Location> moveLocs = new ArrayList<Location>();
    ArrayList<Location> occupiedLocs = myGrid.getOccupiedLocations();

    for (Location loc : occupiedLocs) {
        Actor occupant = myGrid.get(loc);
        if ((! (occupant instanceof TravelerBug)) && (! isVisited(loc))) {
            moveLocs.add(loc);
        }
    }
    return moveLocs;
}
```

Part (b)

```
public void move(List<Location> moveLocs) {
// Precondition: moveLocs is not empty
//
// Choose a random location in moveLocs and move there.
// After moving, add the chosen location to visitedList.

    int index = (int)(Math.random() * moveLocs.size());
    Location newLoc = moveLocs.get(index);
    moveTo(newLoc);
    visitedList.add(newLoc);
}
```

Part (c)

```
public void act( ) {
// Get a list of occupied locations in the grid that do not contain a
// traveler bug, and that this traveler bug has not yet visited.
// If the list is empty, remove this traveler bug from the grid.
// Otherwise, cause this traveler bug to move to one of the locations
// in the list.

    List<Location> moveLocs = getMoveLocs();
    if (moveLocs.size() == 0) {
            removeSelfFromGrid();
    } else {
        move(moveLocs);
    }
}
```

Grading Guide

Part (a) getMoveLocs   5 Points

+ 1   Gets and iterates over occupied locations

    + 1/2   attempt (must attempt to reference the list of occupied locations within the loop)

    + 1/2   correct

+ 1   Correct test for unvisited (can use isVisited or ArrayList contains method)

+ 1   Correct test for occupant is a TravelerBug

+ 2   Correct initialization and return of result array (must add values in the loop)

Part (b) move   2 Points

+ 1   Correctly chooses a random location

+ 1   Correctly calls moveTo, and updates visitedList

Part (c) act   2 Points

+ 1   Correct call to getMoveLocs

+ 1   Correctly handles both empty and non empty list of move locations

Question 2

Part (a)

```
public class LaundryOrder {
   private String name;
   private int numItems;
   private boolean isReady;

   public LaundryOrder(String n, int num) {
      name = n;
      numItems = num;
      isReady = false;
   }

   public String getName() { return name; }
   public int getNumItems() { return numItems; }
   public boolean orderIsReady() { return isReady; }

   public void setIsReady() { isReady = true; }
}
```

Part (b)

```
public class AlterationOrder extends LaundryOrder {
   private String instructions;

   public AlterationOrder(String n, String inst) {
      super(n, 1);
      instructions = inst;
   }

   public String getInstructions() { return instructions; }
}
```

Part (c)

```
public ArrayList<LaundryOrder> unfinishedOrders() {
   ArrayList<LaundryOrder> answer = new ArrayList<LaundryOrder>();
   for (LaundryOrder oneOrder : allOrders) {
      if (!oneOrder.orderIsReady()) answer.add(oneOrder);
   }
   return answer;
}
```

Grading Guide

Part (a) The LaundryOrder class   3 Points

+ 1/2   Declare class LaundryOrder

+ 1/2   Private instance variable declarations

+ 1/2   Constructor

+ 1   Accessor methods

    + 1/2   attempt

    + 1/2   correct

+ 1/2   Method to change state of boolean field

Part (b) The AlterationOrder class   3 Points

+ 1   Declare class AlterationOrder

    + 1/2   attempt (can receive without extends)

    + 1/2   correct

+ 1 1/2   Constructor

    + 1/2   attempt (can receive without super)

    + 1/2   call to super

    + 1/2   correct (including passing 1 for number of items)

+ 1/2   getInstructions

Part (c) unfinishedOrders   3 Points

+ 1/2   Create ArrayList to return

+ 1   Loop over allOrders

    + 1/2   attempt

    + 1/2   correct

+ 1   Check for orderIsReady and add to created ArrayList

    + 1/2   attempt at check

    + 1/2   correct with add

+ 1/2   Return created ArrayList

Question 3

Part (a)

```
private int personBeforePos(int age) {
   for (int pos=0; pos<peopleList.size(); pos++) {
      Person currentPerson = peopleList.get(pos);
      if (currentPerson.getAge() > age) return pos-1;
   }
   // here if all people in the list have ages <= given age;
   // return the position of the last person in the list or
   // -1 if the list was empty
   return peopleList.size()-1;
}
```

Part (b)

```
public void addPerson(Person p) {
   int pos = personBeforePos(p.getAge());
   peopleList.add(pos+1, p);
   // now fix numSameAge fields if necessary
   while (pos >= 0) {
      Person onePerson = peopleList.get(pos);
      if (onePerson.getAge() == p.getAge()) {
         int num = onePerson.getNumSameAge() + 1;
         onePerson.setNumSameAge(num);
         p.setNumSameAge(num);
         pos--;
      } else return;
   }
}
```

Grading Guide

Part (a) `personBeforePos`   4 Points

+ 1   Handle empty list correctly

+ 2   Traverse list to find and return appropriate position

+ 1   Return index of last person when no person is older

Part (b) `addPerson`   5 Points

+ 1   Call to `personBeforePos`

    + 1/2   attempt

    + 1/2   correct

+ 1   Add p at correct position.

    + 1/2   when `personBeforePos` returns -1

    + 1/2   when `personBeforePos` returns another value

+ 3   Update `numSameAge` fields

    + 1   update p's field correctly

    + 1   attempt to update other people's fields (must include a loop)

    + 1   correctly update other people's fields

Question 4

Part (a)

Note that method `willFruit` is much easier to write if you first write an auxiliary method that tests one position of the array to see whether that position is inside the `plants` array and, if so, contains a male plant:

```
private boolean isMale(int row, int col) {
    if (row < 0 || row >= plants.length ||
        col < 0 || col >= plants[0].length) return false;
    return( plants[row][col].equals("male"));
}
```

This auxiliary method is used by both versions of the `willFruit` method given below.

Version 1: Check each position explicitly.

```
public boolean willFruit( Position p ) {
    return(isMale(p.getRow(), p.getColumn()-1) ||
            isMale(p.getRow(), p.getColumn()+1) ||
            isMale(p.getRow()-1, p.getColumn()) ||
            isMale(p.getRow()-1, p.getColumn()-1) ||
            isMale(p.getRow()-1, p.getColumn()+1) ||
            isMale(p.getRow()+1, p.getColumn()) ||
            isMale(p.getRow()+1, p.getColumn()-1) ||
            isMale(p.getRow()+1, p.getColumn()+1) ||
            isMale(p.getRow()+2, p.getColumn()) ||
            isMale(p.getRow()-2, p.getColumn()) ||
            isMale(p.getRow(), p.getColumn()+2) ||
            isMale(p.getRow(), p.getColumn()-2));
}
```

Version 2: Use a loop to check all positions one step away (horizontally, vertically, or diagonally), then check all positions two steps away horizontally or vertically.

```java
public boolean willFruit( Position p ) {
    int r = p.getRow();
    int c = p.getColumn();

    // check one step away
    for (int row=r-1; row<=r+1; row++) {
        for (int col=c-1; col<=c+1; col++) {
            if (isMale(row, col)) return true;
        }
    }

    // check two steps away horizontally or vertically
    return(isMale(p.getRow()+2, p.getColumn()) ||
            isMale(p.getRow()-2, p.getColumn()) ||
            isMale(p.getRow(), p.getColumn()+2) ||
            isMale(p.getRow(), p.getColumn()-2));
}
```

Part (b)

```java
public ArrayList<Position> willNotFruit() {
    ArrayList<Position> L = new ArrayList<Position>();

    for (int j=0; j<plants.length; j++) {
        for (int k=0; k<plants[0].length; k++) {
            if (plants[j][k].equals("female")) {
                Position p = new Position(j,k);
                if (!willFruit(p)) {
                    L.add(p);
                }
            }
        }
    }
    return L;
}
```

Grading Guide

Part (a) `willFruit`   4 Points

+ ½   Correctly access row and column values of position `P` somewhere in method

+ 2   Check one step away

+ ½   attempt to traverse all locations one step away

+ ½   attempt to check for `isMale` of all locations one step away

+ ½   correct

+ ½   return appropriate value for checked positions

+ 1   Check two steps away

+ ½   attempt to traverse all locations two steps away

+ ½   correct

+ ½   Return `true`/`false` correctly based on all searches

Part (b) `willNotFruit`   5 Points

+ ½   Create `ArrayList` to return

+1½   Traverse matrix

+ ½   attempt to traverse rows

+ ½   attempt to traverse columns

+ ½   correct

+ 1   Comparison for female

+ ½   attempt (must compare with value from matrix)

+ ½   correct

+ ½   Create new position

+ ½   Call to `willFruit`

+ ½   Add to `ArrayList` if appropriate

+ ½   Return created `ArrayList`

Glossary

abs. One of the methods of the `Math` class. It returns the absolute value of a given `int` or `double`.

abstract class. A class that cannot itself be instantiated. Its purpose is to define the methods that all of its subclasses must have.

abstract method. A method of an abstract class that must be defined in all subclasses.

actual parameter. One of the values passed when a method is called (see also formal parameter).

add. One of the methods of the `List` interface (and the `ArrayList` class).

argument. Same as actual parameter.

arithmetic operators. `+ - * / %` (addition, subtraction, multiplication, division, and modulus).

ArrayList. One of the AP CS standard Java classes that may be tested on the AP exam. An `ArrayList` implements a list using an array.

assignment operators. `= += -= *= /= %=` (plain assignment, add-then-assign, subtract-then-assign, multiply-then-assign, divide-then-assign, and modulus-then-assign).

base case. Every recursive method must have a base case, which is a condition under which the method does not call itself.

binary search. An efficient technique for finding a value in a sorted array; a value can be found in an array of N elements in time proportional to $\log_2 N$ (see also sequential search).

casting. Used to convert one datatype to another. For example: `int(3.5)` converts the floating-point value 3.5 to an integer (by truncating it to 3).

class. The basic mechanism provided by object-oriented languages to support abstract datatypes.

compareTo. One of the methods of the `String` class. It is used to compare two strings.

compound assignment. `+= -= *= /= %=` (add-then-assign, subtract-then-assign, multiply-then-assign, divide-then-assign, and modulus-then-assign).

constructor. A class's constructor(s) should initialize the fields of the class.

decrement operator. `--` (subtracts one from its operand).

default constructor. A constructor with no arguments.

Double. One of the standard Java classes that may be tested on the AP exam. A `Double` object represents a `double` value.

doubleValue. One of the methods of the `Double` class. it returns the `double` value represented by the `Double` object.

dynamic dispatch. The technique used to determine which version of a method that has been overridden by a subclass is actually called at runtime.

efficiency. How much time and/or space is required by an algorithm or data structure.

equality operators. == and != (equal to and not equal to).

`equals`. One of the methods of the `Object` class. When you define a class, it is usually a good idea to override this method.

enhanced for-loop. See *for-each loop*.

field (nonstatic). A variable associated with each instance of a class (see also instance variable).

field (static). A variable associated with a class (see also instance variable).

for-loop. A loop of the form for (*init-expression*; *test-expression*; *update-expression*) *statement*.

for-each loop. A loop of the form for (*type id1 : id2*) *statement*.

formal parameter. One of the identifiers listed in a method header that corresponds to the values passed when the method is called (see also actual parameter).

generic class or interface. A class or interface that is parameterized by one or more types. Variable declarations supply the type. For example: `ArrayList<String> list;`

`get`. One of the methods of the `List` interface (and the `ArrayList` class).

`if` **statement.** A statement of the form if (*expression*) *statement* or if (*expression*) *statement* else *statement*.

increment operator. ++ (adds one to its operand).

`indexOf`. One of the methods of the `String` class. It returns the index of the first occurrence of a given sequence of characters in the string.

Insertion Sort. A sorting algorithm that takes time proportional to N^2 to sort N items, unless the items are already in sorted order in which case it takes time proportional to N.

instance variable. Another name for a field of a class.

`Integer`. One of the standard Java classes that may be tested on the the AP exam. An `Integer` object represents an `int` value.

interface. Similar to a class, but an interface can only contain public, static, final fields and public, abstract methods. A class can implement one or more interfaces.

`intValue`. One of the methods of the `Integer` class. It returns the `int` value represented by the `Integer` object.

iteration. One execution of the body of a loop.

`length`. For a one-dimensional array A, `A.length` is the length of the array; for a rectangular two-dimensional array A, `A.length` is the number of rows in the array, and `A[0].length` is the number of columns in the array. For a `String` S, `S.length()` is the number of characters in the string.

`List`. One of the AP CS standard Java interfaces that may be tested on the AP exam; a `List` represents an ordered collection of objects. The `ArrayList` class implements the `List` interface.

logical operators. ! && || (logical NOT, logical AND, and logical OR).

`Math`. One of the AP CS standard Java classes that may be tested on the AP exam.

Merge Sort. A sorting algorithm that takes time proportional to $\log_2 N$ to sort N items.

`new` **operator.** Used to create a new instance of an `Object` (it allocates memory from free storage).

`null.` A special value used for a pointer that does not point to any memory location.

`Object.` One of the standard Java classes that may be tested on the AP exam. All Java classes are subclasses of `Object`.

overloading. Defining two versions of a method in the same class with the same name but with different numbers or types of parameters.

overriding. Defining a method in a subclass with the same name, the same numbers and types of parameters, and the same return type as a method in a superclass. Dynamic dispatch is used to determine which version is actually called at runtime. This is one of the *polymorphic* aspects of Java.

parameter. Same as formal parameter.

pointer. A location whose value is another location (a memory address). The computer memory associated with an `Object` holds a pointer to the actual object. Also called a *reference*.

pointer equality. When two pointers are compared using `==` or `!=`, they are considered equal only if they point to the same address; if they point to different addresses that contain the same value, the pointers are considered not equal. Pointer equality is also the default for an object's `equals` method.

pointer parameters. Objects are really pointers, so when an object is passed as a value parameter, although the object itself cannot be changed by the method, the contents of the location that it points to can be changed.

polymorphism. Literally, "many forms." In object-oriented languages like Java, there are several kinds of *polymorphism:* a method with a parameter of type T can be called with an actual parameter of type T or any subtype of T (and that method is a *polymorphic method*), and when a method call of the form *identifier.methodname(parameters)* is executed, if *identifier* is an object, then the method called depends on the runtime type of that identifier (i.e., what kind of object it actually points to) rather than its declared type.

postcondition. A method's postcondition specifies what will be true when the method returns, assuming that the method's preconditions are satisfied when it is called.

`pow.` One of the methods of the `Math` class. It returns the value of the given base raised to the given exponent.

precondition. A method's precondition specifies what is expected to be true whenever the method is called.

`private.` One of the levels of access that can be specified for a class's fields and methods; private fields and methods can only be accessed/called by an instance of the class (see also public).

`public.` One of the levels of access that can be specified for a class's fields and methods; public fields and methods can be accessed/called by a client of the class (see also private).

`random.` One of the methods of the `Math` class. It returns a `double` that is greater than or equal to 0 and less than 1.

recursive method. A method that calls itself (either directly or indirectly).

relational operators. < <= > >= (less than, less than or equal to, greater than, and greater than or equal to).

remove. One of the methods of the List interface (and the ArrayList class).

return **statement.** Executing a return statement causes control to be transferred from the currently executing method to the calling method; for a non-void method, a return statement is also used to return a value.

return type. The type returned by a non-void method.

Selection Sort. A sorting algorithm that takes time proportional to N^2 to sort N items, even if the items are already in sorted order.

sequential search. An algorithm that looks for a value in an array by starting with the first element and examining each element in turn; it requires time proportional to the size of the array on average (see also binary search).

set. One of the methods of the List interface (and the ArrayList class).

short-circuit evaluation. Expressions involving the logical AND and OR operators are guaranteed to be evaluated from left to right, and evaluation stops as soon as the final value is known.

size. One of the methods of the List interface (and the ArrayList class).

sqrt. One of the methods of the Math class. It returns the square root of the given double.

static. A field or method of a class associated with the class itself rather than with an instance of the class.

String. One of the AP CS standard Java classes that may be tested on the AP exam. A String represents a sequence of characters.

subclass. A class that extends an existing class. (The subclass should have an "*is-a*" relationship with the class that it extends.)

substring. One of the methods of the String class. It returns a specified part of the string.

superclass. A class that is extended by a new class.

toString. One of the methods of the Object class; converts the object to a string. When you define a class, it is usually a good idea to override this method.

value parameter. In Java, all parameters are passed by value: When a method is called, the actual parameters are copied into new locations (named with the names of the formal parameters); therefore, changes made to the formal parameter by the called method do not change the corresponding actual parameter.

void. The return type of a method that performs an action rather than computing (and returning) a result.

while-loop. A loop of the form while (*expression*) *statement*. A while-loop may execute zero times (see also for-loop).

Index